ST AIDAN'S
WAY OF
MISSION

RAY SIMPSON
WITH BRENT LYONS-LEE

CELTIC INSIGHTS FOR A
POST-CHRISTIAN WORLD

BRF

NOTE ON SOURCES

The main source of information about Aidan's mission is Bede's Ecclesiastical History of the English People. *Translations from the Latin, with extensive notes, include the following editions:*

- *Oxford University Press, edited with introduction by Judith McClure and Roger Collins (1994)*
- *Penguin Classics, advisory editor Betty Radice (1990)*
- *Gutenberg online translation and notes by A.M. Sellar (George Bell and Sons, 1907)*

Bede's Ecclesiastical History *is divided into four books, each with several chapters. References are indicated in the text by the format EH [X = book]. [Y = chapter].*

CONTENTS

INTRODUCTION

In response to the challenge posed by ISIS (or ISIL) to the world, Archbishop Justin Welby said:

> It is also necessary, over time, that any response to ISIL and to this global danger be undertaken on an ideological and religious basis that sets out a more compelling vision, a greater challenge and a more remarkable hope than that offered by ISIL... If we struggle against a call to eternal values, however twisted and perverted they may be, without a better story, we will fail in the long term.[1]

Aidan's seventh-century mission to English-speaking peoples offers a better story, a more compelling vision and a greater challenge than any I know.

The archbishop told a meeting of new monastic communities that he could not see how the churches can bring the gospel to the world because they are so disunited. Their disunity springs from historical circumstances that have no relevance to people today. The only way forward he could see would be through a revival of some kind of monasticism that went deeper than the divisions. Aidan inspires a contemporary missionary monasticism whose roots are older and more organic than Benedict and which can sow seed and bear fruit not just in enclosed places but in the streets of the world.

Winston Churchill said:

> When one generation no longer esteems its own heritage and fails to pass the torch to its own children, it is saying in essence

that the very foundational principles and experiences that make it the society that it is are no longer valid. What is required when this happens and the society has lost its way, is for leaders to arise who have not forgotten the discarded legacy and who love it with all their hearts. They can then become the voice of that lost generation, wooing an errant generation back to the faith of their fathers, back to the ancient foundations and the bedrock values.[2]

Aidan, whose name means 'little flame', calls us to rediscover the best of that legacy and to pass on the torch of faith like Olympic flame bearers who circle the globe.

Although Aidan was a man of a particular time and place, he is archetypal and universal. His bottom-up mission took root and fruited in the English soul. In the 19th and 20th centuries, vast numbers of English-speaking Britons and Irish dispersed across the world, taking with them, whether they knew it or not, something of Aidan in their gene pool. Among the diverse worldwide mission approaches in the centuries that followed Aidan, the top-down approach has often dominated. A paradigm shift requires a new lens by which to look afresh at our Christian narrative. Aidan's Irish mission to the English is not only a great story; it offers a bottom-up model that can transform our time.

INCARNATIONAL AND INDIGENOUS MISSION

ANY COMMUNITY, CHURCH, NATION THAT FORGETS ITS MEMORY BECOMES SENILE.[3]

Mission has become a bad, if not uncomfortable word. It has ridden on the back of colonial conquest. For example, the colonists who settled in Australia created the legal fiction that its indigenous people did not exist, in order to legitimise their conquest. They had a disregard for the spiritual depth of the tribes. Later, they created reservations for Aboriginal people but forcibly 'stole' their children and put them in 'the Mission', which was run by the government or the church. There, the gospel was preached but abuse was modelled.

Hispanic peoples were brought the gospel by members of religious orders who had a Bible in one hand and a sword in the other. These missionaries called the natives 'savages' and required them to renounce their beliefs, good and bad alike, and embrace 'the true faith'. The Anglos in North America took a similar approach, giving rise to the conflict between cowboys and 'Indians'. Some of them preached the gospel but failed to respect either the Native Americans or the earth they cherished. Many Afro-Caribbeans have inherited their faith from forebears who were slaves. The slave owners made sure the gospel was preached to them, but modelled slavery.

We need a new paradigm, for these reasons and, in the broadest sense, because there is now widespread talk of 'the end of Christendom'. One definition of Christendom is 'the church, organised according to the machinery and mindset of empire'. After the Roman emperor Constantine (d.337) had claimed to be a Christian upon seeing a cross in the sky with the words 'In this sign conquer', the church was organised much along the lines of the Roman civil service. Its bishops were enthroned and wore imperial purple and its congregations were clericalised. The mindset continued during the centuries of 'the Holy Roman Empire' (ninth to 18th centuries in varying parts of central Europe) and remains to this day.

Are we post-Christendom? David Edwards begins his book *The Futures of Christianity* with these words: 'Christianity is young and if it lasts for as long as humanity is expected to last on this planet it has futures of at least two thousand million years ahead of it.'[4] The worst thing that could happen would be for the old Christendom to be replaced by a new Christendom emerging from the fast-multiplying churches of Africa, Asia and Latin America. Philip Jenkins alerts us to this danger in *The Next Christendom: The coming of global Christianity*.[5] The prosperity gospel appeals to the poor, but what happens when they have a welfare state? Mass-organisation evangelism by churches in Korea and China are like a giant productivity drive, but they have not worked in Europe's alien culture because they have not been culture-sensitive. They can appeal to governments because of their work ethic. They typically have no time to 'waste with God' in inner transformation of the false ego.

The 'Christendom' or 'colonial' mission instinct also built the tower of Babel. God opposes this and any project to standardise and control. God's response to the tower of Babel was to scatter the people, who developed competing cultures and languages. The coming of the Holy Spirit at Pentecost overcomes the confusion and fragmentation, but it does so (in the words of

Miroslav Volf) 'not by reverting to the unity of cultural uniformity but by advancing toward the harmony of cultural diversity'.[6]

These flawed models have led to a reaction. Liberation theology, rooted in South America, identified God's kingdom among the poor and the powerless. In Africa and Australasia, post-colonial theology is taught. This uses the term 'missional', as do recent evangelistic networks, in order to distinguish their approach from the 'mission' of the colonial era. By the late 1990s in Australia, the Forge network was inspiring pioneering church leaders, and, when Alan Hirsch wrote *The Shaping of the Things to Come* with Michael Frost in 2003,[7] this book became a must-read for any Christian interested in the future of the church. The concept of the *missio Dei* (the mission of God), which is central to their thesis about the church becoming a missional movement again, was drawn from missiologist David Bosch's seminal work.[8]

A major shift also took place within the Church of England, which reverberated throughout other denominations when the *Mission-Shaped Church* report was launched in 2004.[9] Church renewal was taking place already throughout the UK. However, with this report, the experimentation was recognised as not just a fringe concept but absolutely necessary for the future of the church.

A detailed study entitled 'An analysis of fresh expressions of Church and church plants begun in the period 1992–2012' was carried out by the Church Army's Research Unit between January 2012 and October 2013.[10] The researchers spoke to the leaders of 518 fresh expressions in the dioceses of Liverpool, Canterbury, Leicester, Derby, Chelmsford, Norwich, Ripon and Leeds, Blackburn, Bristol and Portsmouth. These dioceses were chosen to reflect variety in context and geographical spread and different stances towards fresh expressions. A fresh expression of church is defined as:

- missional: it serves those outside the church.
- contextual: it listens to people and enters their culture.
- educational: it makes discipleship a priority.
- ecclesial: it forms church.

Canon Dr George Lings, who led the study, said, 'Nothing else in the Church of England has this level of missional impact and the effect of adding further ecclesial communities.'[11] Bishop Graham Cray, Archbishops' Missioner and leader of the Fresh Expressions team, said:

> *This thorough research shows the numerical scale, the demo-graphic spread and the sheer variety of fresh expressions of church in the Church of England. Particularly significant is the proportion of people involved who have never been part of any church in their lifetime, and the number of new lay leaders who have never previously been involved. These findings offer hope and show that the Church of England does know how to draw unchurched people into Christian discipleship and fellowship, and that decline is not inevitable.*[12]

Many missional networks originate in the USA. In popular perception, the empire of recent decades has been US-led capitalism. This has gone worldwide through 'brand imposition' by capitalism's 'hidden persuaders'—open and subliminal advertising that puts product success before the well-being of the producer, the consumer or the society. Some emerging evangelistic networks, perhaps without being aware of it, use essentially the same approach, aiming to reach the greatest number in the shortest time with a product—the product being Jesus, presented in their own unique format. This must be the right approach, they argue, because it registers the highest response rate. John Drane has called this approach 'the McDonaldisation of the Church'.[13]

There is a danger that mission is divorced from justice and the bedrock values that create community, and that the short term is divorced from the long term. Both ISIL and Pepsi Cola have a mission: what decides their worth are the values upon which their mission is based.

In the light of these challenges, we now look at the seventh-century Aidan Way of Mission to see if we can learn from its components and credentials.

THE AIDAN WAY OF MISSION

Pagan Ireland had become 'a land of saints and scholars'. It was said that great St Columba alone had founded 300 seven-days-a-week faith communities, whose mother community was across the sea on the island of Iona. The Irish, who were known as Scots, had colonised a western section of the land now named after them—Scotland. Iona was part of this colony, which they named Dalriada. Columba had sailed from Iona to anoint its king in the name of Christ at his fortress on the Rock of Dunadd.

Columba had a passion for evangelism. It was said that his soul friend had urged him to win as many souls to Christ in a foreign land as had been lost in a battle between his tribe and another. Once, Columba made the long trek up the Great Glen beside Loch Ness to befriend the pagan Pictish king Bruid. On the way, he commanded a monster Loch Ness fish, which had attacked fishermen, to depart in the name of Christ. This it did until the modern tourist industry revived interest in the Loch Ness monster. Columba prayed for a sick member of King Bruid's family and began to evangelise the Picts.

Columba died in 597, about the time that Aidan was born. Aidan joined Columba's family of monasteries. We don't know where or when, but we presume he was steeped in Irish monastic ways— genuine, close to the people, soaked in scripture, hospitable in his zeal to live and share the gospel. Many of Columba's monks came from his Ui Neill tribe and many of the abbots who succeeded him were related to its chief, Conall Gulban. Perhaps Aidan was, too.

About the time when Aidan was most probably posted to Iona, concern grew among the Christian Dalriadans about the pagan Anglo-Saxon colonists who had established their largest kingdom on Dalriada's southern border—a kingdom known as Northumbria. Northumbria's rival kings constantly slew each other. One of them, Edwin, married a princess from Kent who had become a Christian through the mission sent there from Rome by Pope Gregory. She brought her Italian chaplain, Bishop Paulinus, with her. Edwin became a Christian and summoned his subjects to royal centres to hear Paulinus. He baptised thousands in various rivers. These conversions had an effect: it was said that a boy could run from one end of the kingdom to the other without being molested. Yet, when Edwin was slain, Paulinus fled to Kent and most of the converts went back to their pagan gods. The mission had been a firework display. The people had accepted the externals of the new religion but they were not changed from within.

Edwin's predecessor, Ethelric, had been killed by Edwin's ally. Ethelric's boys, the legitimate heirs, took refuge, with family and staff, in Christian Dalriada. They were adopted by treaty and became Christians. The most devout of them, Oswald, used to rise early to pray with his hands open to heaven. He regained the Northumbrian throne following a year of ghastly bloodshed. He asked Iona to send a mission to his mostly pagan people, but it failed.

It seems that Corman, the mission leader, made the same mistake as Paulinus. He expected ordinary peasants to come to royal centres. They found themselves in a foreign place, with a foreign person using a foreign language. He told them about a foreign religion that required them to accept foreign ways; and, unlike Paulinus, he did not even dazzle them with hints of a Christianity of future pomp and circumstance. Corman's mission team returned to Iona and blamed the uncouth Northumbrians for its failure.

The Iona brothers were devastated. This was the greatest missed mission opportunity in their history—but then came a surprise from the God of surprises. Oswald asked them to try once more. Their senior brothers met in council under Seghine, Iona's fifth abbot. This was not only a post-mortem: in the brokenness of failure they sought to learn God's lessons. Aidan spoke. 'My brother,' he said to Corman, 'I think you were too harsh with those people. It is better not to lay on them our own rules and ways of doing things. Just gently give them the milk of God's word.' Was he thinking of milk from within a mother's breast being imbibed by her infant? The milk of God's word mixed with the milk of human kindness: thirsty people would not resist that.

So Aidan was sent to Northumbria with twelve brothers, based, as was usual in Irish missions, on the template of Jesus and his twelve apostles. He must have given careful thought, in the light of the first mission's failure to connect, to the kind of brothers he should select for his team. They had to be strong enough to connect with the Saxon warrior culture and to walk long distances, yet they also had to be gentle, open to listening, patient and adaptable. Doubtless, among the gifts he looked for in his team were those of teaching, friendship, practical skills and devotion to prayer. Aidan was already a senior monk and a presbyter. Now (unless we believe the Scattery Island version) he was also made a missionary bishop, because he was entering uncharted territory and this position would give him the church's authority to exercise oversight.

In 635, Aidan and his twelve 'apostles' journeyed south and crossed over into Northumbria, crossing from one race, one religion and one language to another. He gave the rest of his life to incarnate Christ among foreign peoples—the pagan Anglo-Saxons and the remnants of the Celtic Britons who had survived the invaders and who spoke what we now call Welsh.

Aidan came, like the two previous missioners, with a message, but unlike them he also modelled the message. He did this in two ways: first, by living a way of life that reflected gospel values, and second, by creating little 'colonies of heaven' that modelled something of the kingdom of God on earth. He did not rush out where angels fear to tread. He built up a relationship of trust with his sponsor, King Oswald, and with Oswald's staff and warriors. He had learned some English from the royal refugees at Dunadd, but, until he was fluent, Oswald, with great humility, translated as Aidan shared the gospel at the court.

Aidan, however, was keen to go into the highways and byways. His plan met an early hurdle that could have aborted the mission before it had begun. Oswald gave him a royal horse. No doubt Oswald thought this was fitting for a bishop and would enable Aidan to reach the greatest number in the shortest time. Aidan, however, wished to walk alongside his missionary brothers and alongside the peasants who could not afford horses. This was what Jesus had done on the paths of Judea. To ride a horse would put him above ordinary people and create a cultural divide. Risking Oswald's anger, he refused the royal gift.

With a few brothers, Aidan traversed both town and country on foot. The travellers turned aside to greet anyone they met, whether poor or rich, listening to them and becoming friends. If the people they met were believers, the brothers strengthened them in the faith and stirred them up, by words and actions, to the giving of alms and the performance of good works. They asked unbelievers if they would like to know why they had come, and told them Gospel stories.

At the Iona post-mortem on Corman's failed mission, Corman had put its failure down to the barbaric nature of the Northumbrians. Aidan had argued that the missioners should have been more gentle and should have only gradually laid down the whole gamut of Christian teachings. Bede (the monk-historian who recorded these events some 50 years later) commended Aidan's tenderness in comforting the afflicted and relieving the poor, living what he taught: 'He took care to neglect none of those things which he found in the Gospels and the writings of apostles and prophets, but to the utmost of his power endeavoured to fulfil them all in his deeds' (*EH* 3.17).

This approach had a deep effect. Two decades after Aidan's death, Bede could record:

> *Wherever a missionary brother went, he was joyfully received by all as God's servant; and even if they chanced to meet him upon the way, they ran to him, and with bowed head, were glad to be signed with the cross by his hand, or blessed by his lips. Great attention was also paid to their exhortations. (EH 3.5)*

The result was they had to send for more Irish missioners, who arrived almost daily. A sea-change was under way. A grass-roots revolution had begun.

MISSION NEEDS TO BE INDIGENOUS

Aidan's aim was to develop an indigenous, English-speaking church. In Britain and Ireland, none of the pre-Saxon Celtic Christian missionaries who won over the indigenous population were martyred. This was because they were able to contextualise and see where God was already at work. Celtic Christians incorporated insights from the druids who had the wisdom of nature. The druids had a deep intuition. There is an Irish story that, on the day of Christ's crucifixion, King Conchubar noticed the eclipse of the sun and asked the druid Bucrach the cause of this sign. 'Jesus Christ, the Son of God, who is now being crucified by the Jews,' replied the druid.

As a baptised boy, Columba was taught by a druid; as an adult he supported measures to strengthen the institution of the bards, yet he tried to lead both druids and their pupils to Christ. 'Christ is my druid,' he told them. Celtic believers Christianised the pagan seasons. The pagan blessing of the lustral waters on 6 January became a commemoration of Jesus' immersion in the waters. Candles were held to the throat for healing on the first day of the Celtic spring, and this became St Brigid's Day. Christians continued the druids' use of ashes as a sign of purification. The veil between earth and heaven was said to be at its thinnest on Samhain, the first day of winter's dark: Christians filled it with the splendour of All Saints' Day.

An example of Jesus being introduced to an indigenous people with a sensitivity similar to that shown by Aidan can be seen from an Aboriginal people in the Daly Bridge region of Australia's Northern Territory. In *Dadirri: The Spring Within*, Miriam-Rose Ungunmerr-Baumann writes, 'There are deep springs within each of us. Within this deep spring, which is the very spirit of God, is a sound. The sound of Deep calling to Deep. The sound of the word—Jesus.'[14] This book quotes an Aboriginal person:

> *In our own way we understood what the Fathers and Sisters were telling us about Jesus, but He lived in a far away country and moved among white people dressed in strange clothes. This was what we saw in pictures, in books and in statues in the Church. Why couldn't He be like us? Why couldn't His country be our country? Now is the time to make the Christian truths our own. We do not want to change those truths but we want to explain them in a way that makes them real to us. Hence our paintings that take the place of words. We have not been told to paint in the way we have. It is from our hearts.*[15]

In Australia, some Aboriginal dreaming stories have amazing connections to the Christian message. Certain tribes were familiar with the kind of stories that the Christian missionaries told and, in some cases, they were awaiting the arrival of a 'redeeming son' or a 'great resurrection'. One example of this is provided by Jerry Jangala, who is responsible for the Emu dreaming story in Warlpiri country. In this story, the flying emu has a redemptive purpose and is resurrected. Jerry makes the easy connection to Jesus when he talks about this story of his people, claiming that 'Jesus is a flying emu'.

Their Way: Indigenous Christianity among the Warlpiri people,
by Ivan Jordan,[16] gives inspiring examples of this approach.
Jordan argues that no one need change cultures to be a Christian.
Looking at Acts 15, if the requirement of circumcision had
prevailed, Christianity would have become no more than a sect
of Judaism. 'Uncle' Rex of the Warlpiri people in the Northern
Territory of Australia says, 'The Bible fits our culture in Western
Australia and Jukurppa—the law of our culture.'

Ethnically mixed areas in our cities cry out for the Aidan
approach. Stories circulate of thousands of Muslims in certain
Arab countries who became followers of Jesus and joined a
church. The church members offended the new believers by not
removing their shoes and placing their Bibles on the floor (both
signs of disrespect), so thousands also left these churches. The
Aidan approach calls out for churches in ethnically mixed areas
that worship in Muslim style: they have carpets, remove shoes
and hold Bibles aloft. It is interesting that the Lindisfarne Gospels,
a rich fruit of Aidan's mission, draw their carpet pages from the
same oriental tradition that marks Muslim art. Michelle Brown
points out that Northumbrian, Celtic and Byzantine monks all
used to pray on decorated prayer carpets, known as *oratorii*, just
as Muslim and certain Eastern Christian Churches have always
done and still do.[17] Perhaps the Aidan approach also calls for
Christians to use prayer mats?

Alan Roxburgh, in his book *Missional: Joining God in the
neighbourhood*, writes:

> *The Spirit is breaking apart a form of church that took shape
> in the Protestant West from the sixteenth century forward...
> God is on the move. The kingdom is so much bigger than our
> little, tribal cultural enclaves, and the world is in crisis. The
> Lord of creation is out there ahead of us, he has left the temple
> and is calling the church to follow in a risky path leaving behind
> its baggage, becoming like the stranger in need, and receiving*

hospitality from the very ones we assume are the candidates for
our evangelism plans. Luke re-theologising would say that the
only way we can understand and practise again this kingdom
message is by getting out of our churches and re-entering our
neighbourhoods and communities. This is where we will discern
God's future, not in our vision and mission statements or the
arrogant need to start a movement in our own image. This is a
time for a radical shift in the imagination and practices of our
once dominant Euro-tribal churches.[18]

Ross Langmead, in *The Word Made Flesh: Towards an incarnational*
missiology, points to three interpretations of incarnational mission:
(1) follow the patterns Jesus used in the Gospels; (2) participate
in Christ's risen presence with us in our context; (3) join God's
cosmic mission of enfleshment in which God's self-embodying
dynamic is evident from the beginning of creation.[19]

REFLECTION

I imagine Aidan training his younger brothers to become culture-
friendly by deep listening to those Saxon peasants whom Corman
had dismissed as barbarians. Pat Loughery, Adjunct Instructor at
The Seattle School of Theology & Psychology, who lectures on
Celtic Spirituality and follows the Community of Aidan and Hilda
Way of Life, asks his students to sit on a park seat and listen while
someone tells their story. He says it has become a fun challenge
to ask his students to listen to other people tell their stories, and
also to try to discern the stories that the culture is telling as a
whole.[20] A Scottish training course for youth workers invites
them to listen to music that young people like or to photograph
street graffiti and draw out what speaks of a longing for God, of
dysfunction because of the flouting of God, or of recognition of
good and therefore godly values. Try one of these exercises.

I imagine Aidan thinking how best to get inside the Saxons'
culture and redeem it. Young Western people often have a pagan

mentality that is drawn to the supernatural; symbols include vampire films and tarot card readings. A church led by a member of The Community of Aidan and Hilda has a youth bus that shows films on the top deck and gives one-on-one spiritual readings on the lower decks, by drawing out information and combining it with perceptive prayer. What are our cultural symbols? How can we baptise them?

I imagine Aidan saying, 'We must move on from the "We are right; you are wrong" approach.' Corman was sure he was right and the Northumbrians were wrong. The Northumbrians had much yet to learn about God, but Corman had much yet to learn about cross-cultural mission. The Pharisees took Corman's approach. Many of the numerically successful churches fall prey to a message that says, 'You are lost and a target of God's wrath. We have Jesus who saves you. Come to Jesus.' The veiled message is, 'We are right; you are wrong.' These Christians' emotional security lies in their being right. There is no room for questions. 'We are right; you are wrong' churches may be judged by their fruit—immaturity and divisions. Members of churches based on Jesus' values become more loving; they make friends with people who don't think like them; they are more attentive and more in touch.

Is your approach more like Jesus' or more like that of the Pharisees who condemned him? Is it about God whipping people or wooing them? A different kind of security from that of the 'We are right' school comes when we say to the triune God of love, 'You have me; you have them.' Then we can let go of what we are holding on to. We are free to meet people in their humanity and to let God do his work his way. This has authority to rally the soul. Proselytism is about converting A to B, and it requires pressure. Evangelism is about bearing witness to Jesus and letting the Holy Spirit lead A, and it requires trust. How do you respond to these two approaches?

I imagine Aidan saying, 'Notice the ways God uses the different characteristics of the first twelve apostles. No two meetings are the same.' Many groups have based missional initiatives on the number of the apostles. The G12 network, started in 1983 by Pastor Castellanos, believes that every Christian can mentor and lead twelve people in the gospel, and then that group can subdivide and repeat the process. The network now claims to have 45,000 cells. In mission that reflects the dynamic of Jesus and the twelve apostles, however, it is not just the number that is important: the spirit is even more so. No two groups should be identical in their approach because God has made each one unique. The group needs to do and say whatever the loving, seeing heart of Jesus directs. The standardised approach is not like milk uniquely given from a mother at the other's moment of need; it is like milk pumped from a machine. Nevertheless, 'the world has yet to see what God can do through twelve people wholly given to him' (Frank Buchman).[21] Recall a saying of Jesus to a needy person that you might describe as giving milk. Empathise with Jesus' compassion for that person as he speaks the words. Focus on the milk of human kindness in yourself. In your imagination, speak a Gospel word to someone out of that milk of kindness.

I imagine Aidan saying, 'Look for Christ in the welcoming heart of a stranger.' Aidan did not bang his head against a door; he went through the door that opened. Jesus said, in effect, 'Go where you are welcomed' (see Luke 10:8). Become aware of what God is already doing in a place and support it. Become aware of doors that are opening, and try them. Oswald's invitation was the opening door, and Aidan needed to build a good relationship with the door opener. What is God already doing in your context? Who are the door openers? How can you support what God is doing?

What are the marks of Aidan's mission by which we may evaluate today's missional models? What are your mission priorities?

Set us free, O God, to cross barriers for you,
as you crossed barriers for us.
Make us open to others in listening,
observant of others in learning,
and sensitive to others in living,
through Jesus Christ our Lord.

CHRISTIAN LIFE: A PILGRIMAGE, NOT A POSSESSION

TRAVEL IN PERPETUAL PILGRIMAGE AS GUESTS OF THE WORLD.

COLUMBANUS

Possessiveness closes up the church; pilgrimage opens it up. Pilgrimage helps us to step off the treadmill and move forward, intent on finding God. 'Blessed are those… whose hearts are set on pilgrimage,' wrote the author of Psalm 84 (v. 5, NIV). A life-changing spiritual dynamic lies hidden in pilgrimage, for, to do it, we have to let go of being in control. For the Irish, pilgrimage was a metaphor for a life. Columba's friend and namesake Columbanus of Bangor, the Irish monk who re-evangelised parts of Europe in the sixth century, wrote in the fifth of his published sermons:

What are you, human life?
You are the road to life, not life itself.
You are a real road but not a level one.
Long for some, short for others,
Broad for some, narrow for others,
Joyful for some, sad for others,

23

For all alike, fleeting and irrevocable.
A road is what you are, a road,
But you are not clear to all.
Many see you
And few understand you to be a road.
For you are so wily and enticing
That few know you are a road.
Therefore you are to be questioned
But not believed and given bail.
You are to be traversed but not inhabited...
For no one dwells on a road, but travels it
So that those who walk upon the road
May dwell in their homeland.[22]

Some of the Irish *peregrini* (lifelong pilgrims) got into boats and allowed the wind to blow them where it wished. They made no separation between God's wind the Holy Spirit, and God's wind in nature.

The Christian church was birthed in a pilgrimage. Pilgrims from many races flocked to Jerusalem for the Pentecost festival (Acts 2:5–11). They had an unforgettable experience, received the gospel and were baptised, thus ensuring that, from its start, Christianity was an international movement of people who travelled with God.

Pilgrimage is at the centre of the Old Testament. Its main focus (in the book of Exodus) is the journey of Moses' people for 40 years through deserts towards a land promised by God. The three great Jewish festivals of Passover, Pentecost and Harvest remember and learn from this pilgrim experience. Thousands of people travelled great distances to be at one of these festivals, Jesus among them. They also spent a week each year living outside their houses in cabins made of tree branches (for the Festival of Booths). The purpose was that they would continue to travel with God inwardly, in their hearts.

Scholars claim that Europe was converted more by the Irish pilgrims, for the love of God, than by the official church missions.[23] These Irish pilgrims did not go to a famous place and return to their familiar homes. Sometimes they set out without knowing where God would lead them, and they lived like this for the rest of their lives. These lifetime pilgrims were also known as white martyrs, because they left their home comforts for ever. To distinguish them from those who go on a short pilgrimage today, scholars retain the Latin word for pilgrims, *peregrini*.

Pilgrimage has become popular again, with more than 200,000 people walking the Camino de Santiago alone in 2014. Ben Edson is an Anglican priest in Manchester who founded one of the earliest fresh expression communities, Sanctus1. In his current role as Vicar of St James and Emmanuel, he is integrating missional communities and has created a dispersed community of prayer and mission called Peregrini, which draws inspiration from the Irish wandering monks and their 'five rhythms of grace'. This phrase is taken from Eugene Peterson's paraphrase of Matthew 11:28: 'Walk with me and work with me—watch how I do it. Learn the unforced rhythms of grace' (*THE MESSAGE*).

AIDAN'S PILGRIMAGE

Aidan, like Columba before him, left his homeland to lay down his life for the English-speaking peoples, never to return. He went into exile from his familiar home. He, too, was one of the *peregrini*. He walked everywhere, and walking, too, is a metaphor for life. Aidan's buildings were provisional, short-lived wooden structures that were easily dismantled once they had outlived their usefulness. The heart of Aidan's mission lay in acquiring not material but spiritual capital. He invited people to journey with their Lord.

Aidan and his faith-sharing teams resisted the temptation to stay in their comfort zones. They journeyed to all the four types of people who made up Northumbria. Bede records the welcome that Aidan's mission brothers received once they had broken through initial barriers, but it seems likely, in the nature of the case, that they first had to overcome hostility in several quarters. 'Once bitten, twice shy' might have characterised the Saxons who had professed conversion under Paulinus and then returned to their pagan gods. Such people are the most difficult to win. Occasionally Aidan's mission met Saxons who still believed. Then there were Britons, mostly poorer people who maintained the local economy as employees of the Saxon incomers. They no doubt resented the Irish brothers, their foreign king and his friend, Aidan. Some of them were pagans, but their Celtic paganism was very different from that of the Saxons. Others had a Christian folk memory. Although they now had no scriptures or priests, they could perhaps recall Gospel stories told by their grandparents. For the new missionaries, this was like teaching grandmother to suck eggs.

None of these four groups were easy to connect with. A meaningful encounter required Aidan's missioners to accompany the movements of these people's hearts and mind with suppleness. If Aidan and his team had not believed that they should keep moving beyond the safe confines of their home base, these people might never have been evangelised (*EH* 1.34).

The pilgrimage model is about making neither faith nor church a possession. In the context of mission, this has profound implications. If we have no permanent home here, we do not empire-build. It is also about letting mission take 'as long as it takes'. In 1997, the churches organised a pilgrimage by coach from Rome via Canterbury to Iona. Its purpose was to celebrate the 1300th anniversary of Columba's death on Iona and Augustine's arrival in Canterbury to convert the English. A friend of mine, a Youth With A Mission worker, did the opposite. He walked solo from Iona to Canterbury. 'More evangelism took place on that pilgrimage than at any time in my life,' he told me.

The reason was that every walker he passed had time to talk. When they learned the reason for his walk, they asked questions. The longing in their hearts for the God they had not named found expression.

One church leader says that his congregation has two types of people: 'position' people, who know what their position is and are against receiving from anyone who does not hold it, and 'boom and bust' people, who have an experience of the Spirit and then take time out when it goes wrong. He wants to bring a third sort into being—the person on a journey who receives from God and mentors others.

In many churches, the focus of time and energy is on mainten-ance of a programme or building. This produces overload, so that any new leads from God are blocked out. In a Celtic-style church, programmes and buildings are provisional; they flow out of Spirit-led initiatives, and when that tide ebbs they are beached. Thus, there is space to hear God for the new thing God wants to do. Churches that live this way are not afraid to cross new boundaries. Sometimes this means asking God to show them an opportunity they are meant to take or a need they are meant to respond to.

Alan Hirsch distinguishes between 'communitas', which he defines as a provisional community on the way to something yet to be revealed, and 'community', which may not be open to change. He writes:

The most vigorous forms of community are those that come together in the context of a shared ordeal or those that define themselves as a group with a mission that lies beyond themselves—thus initiating a risky journey. Too much concern with safety and security, combined with comfort and convenience, has lulled us out of our true calling and purpose.[24]

Aidan's pilgrimage model required times of withdrawal as well as of outreach. He regularly went into retreat in a deserted place. Jesus went into the desert before he began his three-year mission so that the false could be sifted from the true. The three temptations he suffered, as recounted in Matthew 4:1–11, were to find his identity in what he did, what he had, or what others said about him. Those are the three primary places in which people in our secular society find their identity. Many people engage in mission who have not entered the pattern of silence, solitude and retreat that is necessary if we are to find our identity in being a child of God. Jesus ministered out of that place of identity with the Father, which he journeyed into and sustained as a result of his times in a deserted place. Aidan also followed that pattern.

PLACES OF RESURRECTION

Although Aidan thought of his life as a perpetual pilgrimage, it did not mean that he was unmindful of place. Stories have come down to us of Irish saints who thought it was vital to die in 'their place of resurrection'. Although we cannot know which of these stories Aidan knew, Bede's story of Cuthbert and his place of resurrection (which will be told in a later chapter) suggests that Aidan imparted this concept to the English.

The story of Findbarr, who died about 633, two years before Aidan's arrival in Northumbria, tells us much.[25] Having founded a series of small communities and mentored many disciples, he settled at Gougane Garra in what is now West Cork. He built beehive monks' cells on islands in the lake on this large estate, which had been bequeathed to him. He assumed he would die there.

One day, however, some former students arrived. They told their esteemed teacher that they knew this was his place of resurrection, but they were confused by contrary indications that it was to be their place of resurrection. Could he help them sort out the muddle and discern God's will? As Findbarr listened to their witness, he knew that they were pure in heart and that Gougane Garra was for them. He gave them his entire estate, upped and left. Walking along the River Lee, he established more little cells and communities, including several in what is now the Republic of Ireland's second city, Cork, above which soar the exquisite spires of St Finbarr's Cathedral.

We can only speculate on the theology that lay behind this belief. The Irish, following New Testament references, believed that, at death, believers 'slept' with Jesus until the general resurrection and judgement. Then they were given their resurrection bodies and put to work in the place to which God had called them, which was now the new earth. So, to them, it was important to be buried in that place.

For Aidan, place was important but it was not the be-all and end-all. What was all-important to him was to be in the right place at the right time. In our mobile society, which may include cremation after careers in different places, the idea of locating one's place of resurrection may seem anachronistic, but is there a deeper truth here that can be a God-given compass to our work? If a Christian seeks to discern to what and where they are called, I sometimes say, 'Let your feet follow your heart until you find your place of resurrection.' As I reflect upon this, I recall the Old Testament concept of *shalom*—harmony between oneself, one's place, one's neighbours, the environment and God. The place of resurrection is the context in which fruit comes as a gift because we are the right person in the right place at the right time. Creativity flows. Connections take place. Synchronicity occurs. Jesus is revealed.

It is no accident that the risen Christ asked his disciples to meet him first in Galilee. This was 'outside the box'—a place not constrained by life-draining institutional power games. However, he also asked them to meet him in Jerusalem, inside a room that was locked for fear of the Jewish religious authorities. In order to know our place of resurrection, we have to become free of power games. Then, when we are truly free, we can dare to enter a lion's den.

Members of The Community of Aidan and Hilda use the picture of setting sail in the ocean of God's love and of abandoning ourselves to God in the waves of life, when we make vows. A leader of the Community says to the new 'Voyager':

God is calling you to leave behind everything that stops you setting sail in the ocean of God's love. You have heard the call of the Wild Goose, the untameable Spirit of God: be ready for the Spirit to lead you into wild, windy or well-worn places in the knowledge that God will make them places of wonder and welcome.

Pilgrimage is the opposite of driven mission, yet it enables mission in the deepest sense, for it provides welcoming space for the questions of the heart. The scriptures remind us that we have no lasting city on this earth (Hebrews 13:14). Jesus did not say, 'I have come to start a new religion' but 'I have come to bring life.' He says this to people of all religions and races. To them also he says, 'I am the way.' The epistles call us to put on the shoes of peace (Ephesians 6:15). They tell us that this change of lifestyle is as simple as a change of clothes (Colossians 3:9–10).

REFLECTION

I imagine Aidan in his later years, when he spent longer periods in York, tossed from pillar to post between the agendas of Kings Oswy and Oswin, pining for the carefree family life of his childhood in Ireland or for a little hermitage like that on Iona or Farne Isle to which he could retire. Surrounded in York by signs of comfort and grandeur, he could so easily have slid imperceptibly but inexorably into a life cut off from the most needy. I imagine that, as he walked past York's old Roman fort, he was told how the locals had hailed Constantine as the next emperor of the West, when his father Constantius died there amid Rome's ninth legion. I imagine that, as Aidan passed the wooden baptistery where Hilda and Edwin, her great-uncle, were baptised on Easter Day 627, and saw the stone church that Edwin began and Oswald completed in 640, he began to wonder. All things Roman seemed so grand and impregnable. Celtic Christians had long regarded York as a sanctuary during the Anglo-Saxon invasions. They called it Caer Ebruac, *caer* meaning 'a place of refuge', but, since Edwin made it his capital in 312, that had all gone. Aidan heard voices that said, 'Follow York's example: develop impressive buildings that will last.' He resisted these voices. He would be at home in different contexts without judging them, but he would remain true to himself and continue to walk among the people in his simple attire.

Perhaps he did not see the smile on God's face. God knew that, in fact, the Vikings would obliterate all traces of Roman Christian buildings before a century was out. I imagine Aidan walking the Roman walls and encircling its people in prayer. He could resist such temptations to comfort and pomp because he had committed himself to be a pilgrim for the love of God for the rest of his life.

Why did Jesus ask people to follow a way? Why were the first Christians called Followers of the Way? What are the implications for us of being followers? What are its implications for mission? If leaders in mission get their buzz from influencing and controlling others, rather than from a deep sense of gift, this is not their place of resurrection. Step aside; go to Galilee places and allow the purifying Spirit to bring further inner transformation; then respond to call, not compulsion.

What lulls us out of our true calling and purpose? What do we need to let go of? Allow yourself to be who you are in the place you are now, at one with God.

His love that burns inside me impels me on the road
to seek for Christ in the stranger's face
or feel the absence of His touch.[26]

Help us to carry forward Aidan's torch of flame—
Christ, the Light of the world—
in the gentle touch,
in the listening ear,
in the patient toil,
in the concern for the poor,
in the challenging of wrong,
in the next step of the journey of life.

SOUL FRIENDS AND LIFELONG LEARNING

WITH DISCIPLES YOU CAN BUILD MOVEMENTS. WITH CONSUMERS YOU CAN BUILD NOTHING.[27]

Pagan Ireland, it was said, became a land of saints and scholars. Soul friends kept alive people's love of holiness and learning. We do not know whether there was a soul friend tradition, dimmed but still alive, among the Celtic Britons within Northumbria. The Welsh word for soul friend is *periglour*, meaning a person who will allow me to tell the whole truth about myself and to seek healing. We do know that the tradition was burgeoning in Ireland.

Aidan grew up in Columba's family of monasteries, which were steeped in the soul friendship tradition. Columba's friend Comgall, the sixth-century founder of the monastery at Bangor, stated, 'Though you may think you are very solid, it is not good to be your own guide.' His large community taught that 'a person without a soul friend is like a body without a head'.[28]

As I have mentioned, Columba's Iona monastery came into being as a result of his soul friend's advice that he should win as many people to Christ in a foreign land as had lost their lives in the battle between his tribe and another in Ireland. Adomnan's *Life of Columba* cites examples of advice and prophecies that Columba gave, both as a soul friend and more generally.

On one occasion, however, two lads whom Columba had baptised revealed dysfunctional behaviour patterns, and he asked his nephew, Colman, to become their soul friend. Colman was the founder of a monastic village at Land Ela (now Lynally) in central Ireland. He was compared with John the beloved disciple, who laid his head against Jesus at their last supper and to whom Jesus bequeathed his mother as he was dying, thus causing Celts to call him Jesus' foster brother.

Upon receiving Columba's request, Colman said, 'Give them to me to foster and nourish, for God has given me two paps, a pap of milk and a pap of honey, and I will give one to each.' So they, along with others, became his fosterlings. Colman was tough and a friend of the king's chief warrior, but in our language we would say he was in touch with his 'inner feminine'. This image suggests the soul friend as the midwife of souls.

There are two threads in the ancient Irish soul friendship tradition—the provision of fosterers for young people and the provision of soul friends by monasteries. The foster parent was not, as in today's society, a substitute for the physical parents, but was a cherished supplement, who might be widowed or unmarried. The foster parent would not live with the family, as would a modern nanny; the child would stay with the foster parent for periods. As children shared in the life of the foster parent, they might learn to cook, fish, pray, repeat stories, make relationships and grow confident in both practical living and their inner life.

As Christianity spread, Christian parents would sometimes sense that a child was being called to a spiritual vocation, so they would place the child under the care of a holy hermit or nun who lived in their district. A good foster parent would be both worldly-wise and spiritually wise. In sixth-century Ireland, future Christian leaders went to be mentored by a monastic *amma* or *abba* (an affectionate name for a spiritual mum or dad), who taught the wisdoms of scripture, prayer and community in a monastery that combined holy learning with holistic living.

In the early days of the monasteries, there was such trust and desire to move along God's path that a trainee monk was expected to pour out his soul each day to the senior monk who was his soul friend; in this way, things that clogged relationships with God or the brothers could be confessed and forgiven. It is thought that these monks also became soul friends to many people outside the monasteries who were keen to follow God in their ordinary jobs. Both the foster parents and the monastic forms of soul friendship kindled warm bonds of human affection.

St Brigid told a young priest in fifth-century Ireland that, just as the water in a well full of lime was good for nothing, so was a person without a soul friend. Ciaran, who later founded the Clonmacnoise community, first went to be mentored under Finnian of Clonard. Soon after he had established the Clonmacnoise community, Ciaran caught the plague and lay dying. They fetched his soul friend, Kevin, from Glendalough to be with him in death. Kevin seemed to have arrived too late, but Ciaran's spirit re-entered his body. The two friends communed together from one watch to another and Ciaran gave his bell to Kevin as a sign of their lasting unity.

Maedoc founded a seventh-century community at Ferns, Ireland. Many came for spiritual direction, and many went on from there to be soul friends to others. Maedoc first tried to discern whether Ferns was to be their place of resurrection, so he asked them, 'Did any of you hear a bell ring when you arrived?' They did not. Maedoc sensed that, although Ferns did not ring a bell, their place of resurrection would be somewhere within the region to which they had been drawn, so he walked with them to a rise from which they could see miles of countryside around. Speaking out what the Spirit put in his mind, he pointed in each of the compass points in turn. No bell rang. So he told them that they should keep walking until they came to a place that rang a bell.

In Aidan's Ireland, the desire to become holy, to pursue learning and to find a soul friend had become a popular passion. Aidan, like all the brothers at Iona, was allocated a soul friend. Yet much of this was alien to the Anglo-Saxons. How on earth could Aidan crack this hard nut? He modelled it himself and among the monastic communities and schools that he founded for Anglo-Saxons. This was not in the Roman tradition of the monk Bede, who records the bare outlines of Aidan's mission without a mention of soul friends; but it shines out in his account of the life of Cuthbert, the first great Anglo-Saxon church leader and a firstfruit of Aidan's mission, who loved holiness, learning and his soul friend.

After ministry as a prophetic evangelist, healer and prior, Cuthbert lived for nine years as a hermit prayer warrior on the Inner Farne Isle, and then two years as a missionary bishop who planted the church in the shadow of the Rock of Edinburgh. Throughout that time, he was soul friend to the hermit Herbert, who lived on an island in Derwentwater, in today's English Lake District. Each year Herbert trekked from west to east to meet with Cuthbert. Once, Cuthbert met Herbert while on a visit to Carlisle. He urged Herbert to say everything he would wish to say before departing this life, since Cuthbert sensed that his own death was near and this would be their last meeting. Herbert wept and asked Cuthbert to pray that they would each depart to their place of resurrection on the same day. This they did, on 20 March 687.

As the churches in the West became more Romanised, soul friendship became clericalised, and therefore male. Confession of sins became a formal procedure that could be made only to a priest. The Reformation churches did not enforce the practice of confession to a priest, but they failed to rekindle the soul friendship tradition. The Eastern Orthodox churches never entirely lost the tradition of the elder or the holy mother—or, in Russia, the *staretz*—to whom Orthodox Christians could bare their souls as to a trusted friend.

CONTEMPORARY SOUL FRIENDS

The use of spiritual directors, both male and female, began to grow in Roman Catholic and Anglican churches in the 20th century. Today, when life coaches and mentors are in great demand, the soul friend tradition is reviving. A Welsh Franciscan writer, Brother Ramon, sensed the emergence of a vocation to soul friendship among lay folk.[29] After talking it through with him shortly before his death, I wrote *Soulfriendship: Celtic insights into spiritual mentoring*, which explores this vocation further.[30]

Members of an Alpha course decided that, as new Christians, they wished to continue discipleship training but not to join a conventional church, so they formed an Alpha café church. Those who had been leaders during the Alpha course, who were at home with their Bibles and with biblical prescriptions, became 'table leaders' of the café church. Their job now was to intuit where the new Christians on their table were in their unique inner journey and to accompany them. A despairing overseer of these table church leaders came to see me, saying, 'Can you teach people how to get in touch with their intuition and to accompany others from where they are?'

A soul friend may seek to discern with you the context that is, or will be, most life-giving for you. It will take into account your calling, the place where you connect most deeply with the environment, the people and God. You may already be in your place of resurrection, but certain things may still need to be put in place. Remember that Jesus' cross was near to his place of resurrection. The place of resurrection is not pain-free, but it is, at the deepest level, in the will of God. The soul friend may help you to accept what cannot be changed, to change what can be, and the wisdom to know the difference.

The Community of Aidan and Hilda has defined a soul friend as follows:

A soul friend helps a person, in one-to-one meetings, to:

- *Grow in their relationship with God and others.*
- *Explore different ways of praying.*
- *Reflect on the inner promptings of the Holy Spirit.*
- *Feed on scripture.*
- *Gain self-awareness.*
- *Find comfort and strength in times of adversity.*
- *Develop their potential as a human being created in the image of God.*
- *Apply the gospel to each area of their life (for example, money, sex and work).*
- *Maintain a good balance of prayer, work and recreation.*
- *Identify how God has led them in the past, reflect on where they are now and discern direction for the future.*

The Community specifically requires each person who follows its Way of Life to journey with a soul friend—a mature Christian friend with whom we openly share our spiritual journey and meet at least twice a year.[31]

'We prefer groups,' say some missional networks. Groups have a useful place, but their members can be held hostage by the demands of the group's least aware ego. Soul friends also have their limitations, of course, but at the least they are an accompanier, a sounding board, a confidante. Choose a soul friend who recognises their limitations.

DISCERNMENT

Discernment is a key ingredient in contemporary soul friendship. Spiritual discernment is to separate distinctly that which is authentic from that which is false. It is the art of finding God's will in the concrete decisions that face us in the maze of life. It is the process by which we examine, in the light of our faith and our experience of God's love, what draws us away from God and what draws us into intimacy with him. As Christians interact with scripture, church, circumstances, creation and inner conviction, they gradually discover what the indicators of the divine will are.

An early Celtic saint named Morgan (better known by his Latin name, Pelagius) taught that we learn the general principles of behaviour that pleases God from the teachings and example of Jesus, such as the honesty and unselfishness taught in the Beatitudes. Many thoughts or actions can be eliminated as not God's will because they are not absolutely honest, pure, unselfish or loving. Pelagius taught that we must be honest with ourselves, recognising clearly those areas of our lives that we have not yielded to Christ. He identifies sins and attitudes that hinder us from discerning God's will.

Pelagius advises us to use reason to weigh up good and bad consequences before we make a decision, pray about our provisional intentions, become willing to do God's will, and sense by listening to our conscience whether the actions we contemplate or have taken bring increasing peace or increasing disquiet. For Pelagius, the soul friend did not foster dependency but liberated discernment in the seeker.

Soul friendship in the Irish tradition could be holistic. St Ita rebuked Brendan for not consulting her on how to make his boat. Can such soul friendship take root more broadly in our societies? Britain, like other countries, has a shortage of young skilled labour. Migrants help to fill the gap, but this is unpopular because so many British-born people lack paid work. In some areas of the country now, three generations of families have never worked. In Germany, apprenticeship schemes are widespread and effective. The provision of enablers who accompany those who have lost the motivation to work could yield rich dividends. My friends Kylie and Sammy Horner use the income from their live music performances to apprentice needy people in Thailand

and India. They teach them to make and mend things and to utilise water. They also care for their souls.

LIFELONG LEARNING

The monastic communities that became the backbone of Ireland from the sixth century included schools. Sir James Ware calculated that there were 164 famous schools,[32] but there were many more smaller ones. All Columba's monasteries of any size had schools; he founded 32 in what is now Scotland. In general, they had a missionary character. The word 'nurseries' might better describe some centres, such as the school of the legendary St Ita, who was known as the foster mother of the saints of Ireland. Here, learning involved personal and holistic mentoring. In the monasteries the scribe was highly valued. He devoted his time to copying and multiplying books. Scribes not only provided the educational tools for each generation of students; they also preserved the memory of their Christian history and theology.

Aidan continued the same basic pattern of including schools in his monastic communities. Each student was given an *anamchara*—a soul friend. Students memorised the 150 psalms, rehearsing them as they walked and reciting them in the church. They learned to read Latin, the living language of educated people in those days, and to write on tablets of wax. They studied the Gospels and were taught the theology of some of the great church and desert fathers. Aidan had to adapt to the new culture. His students came from Anglo-Saxon families known but not necessarily related to the local king, unlike those in Ireland, where all were part of the king's tribal family. Their tutors, initially, were foreigners—the Irish. Nevertheless, the concept of family remained strong, both because the abbot was a parent figure and because children of families linked to their king made their home there.

Aidan founded his base monastic community in 635 on the tidal island of Lindisfarne, a few miles from Bamburgh. Although Bede wished to equate Aidan's diocesan system to that of Augustine of Canterbury, which is based on geographical boundaries rather than peoples, even he concedes that, at Lindisfarne, the bishop lived with his clergy and the abbot with his monks 'after the manner of a household' (*EH* 4.25). Aidan was bishop of a people, not a place. Something of this spirit was reflected on Lindisfarne a generation later, under Cuthbert. Bede writes in chapter 16 of his prose *Life of Cuthbert* that it is both the seat of a bishop and of an abbot. One dwelling place holds both, and all are monks. The bishop exercises his episcopal functions while the abbot rules the monastery. All the priests, deacons, readers, singers and those in other roles, together with the bishop, keep the common Rule.

Lindisfarne was a mission base more than a university, so the sending of bright pupils to study in Ireland began under Aidan and greatly increased in the years following. Bede informs us that after plague ravaged England, some years after Aidan's death, many of 'the nobility, and of the lower ranks of the English nation' went to Ireland, 'either for the sake of sacred studies, or of a more ascetic life; and some of them presently devoted themselves faithfully to a monastic life; others chose rather to apply themselves to study, going about from one master's cell to another'. The Irish 'willingly received them all, and took care to supply them with daily food without cost, as also to furnish them with books for their studies, and teaching free of charge'. The 20-year-old Egbert took Chad and others with him to Ireland (*EH* 3.27).

Aidan himself was a model of lifelong learning, and his practice took root among English people of different backgrounds. Bede noted 'his industry in keeping and teaching the Divine commandments, his power of study'. English children, as well as their elders, were instructed by their (Irish) teachers in study and the observance of monastic discipline (*EH* 3.3).

Bede writes:

*[Aidan's] course of life was so different from the slothfulness
of our times, that all those who bore him company, whether
they were tonsured or laymen, had to study either reading the
Scriptures, or learning psalms. This was the daily employment
of himself and all that were with him, wherever they went; and
if it happened, which was but seldom, that he was invited to the
king's table, he went with one or two clerks, and having taken a
little food, made haste to be gone, either to read with his brethren
or to pray. (EH 3.5)*

This habit of learning took root among all the races and language
groups in the British Isles:

*There are in the island at present, following the number of the
books in which the Divine Law was written, five languages of
different nations employed in the study and confession of the
one self-same knowledge, which is of highest truth and true
sublimity, to wit, English, British, Scottish, Pictish, and Latin, the
last having become common to all by the study of the Scriptures.
(EH 1.1)*

It was after the 664 Synod of Whitby that Chad, 'being consecrated
bishop, began immediately to labour for ecclesiastical truth and
purity of doctrine; to apply himself to humility, self-denial, and
study' (EH 3.28).

When universities were separated from the monasteries in
the second millennium, they gained greater freedom of research
but they also lost something—a holistic understanding of godly
learning that embraces head, heart and hands and whose source
is God. Wisdom is not learned by mere data accumulation or
cerebral analysis. That is why individuals, churches and networks
now thirst to recover wellsprings of wisdom. We may catch from
the Irish a love of learning rather than a love of letters.

Lifelong learning is for everyone, whether they have an academic or a practical orientation. It begins with daily reflection on scripture. We don't treat scripture as a mere recording. We learn about the times and the issues when a particular biblical document was first written, and about the strengths and weaknesses of the characters portrayed. We accept what is called progressive revelation, and we always ask what new insight God was trying to communicate in that situation. Some people find it helpful to think of scripture as a love letter from God, while others try to memorise a verse a day; one person decided to learn New Testament Greek at the age of 80, and another can't read but listens to scripture recordings.

Many find the practice known as *lectio divina*, or godly reading, helpful. This involves a prayerful reading of a scripture passage, with an openness to hearing God speak through it. You may choose any passage that speaks to your present condition, work through a book in the Bible section by section, or follow a lectionary. Read the passage slowly several times. Stop at words or phrases that speak to you, and mull them over. Let them sink in. Ask yourself both 'What do I think about this?' and 'What do I feel about this?' Share your thoughts, feelings, questions and hopes with God as you would with a friend. Make a response—a prayer of commitment, thanksgiving or repentance or a request for help. Then relax and enjoy God's presence for a while. This pattern is sometimes called the four Rs: reading, reflection, response and relaxing.

Lifelong learning may develop further through reflection on creation and the use of creative arts. Jesus taught us to learn by observation: observe the birds and the wild flowers (Matthew 6:26–30). We interpret clouds and winds to predict the weather, so we can learn to interpret deeper, unseen patterns in order to interpret what God is bringing about (Luke 12:54–56). An ancient church catechism ends with the question 'What is the fruit of study?' The answer is 'To perceive the eternal Word of God reflected in every plant and insect, every bird and animal, and every man and woman.' Meister Eckhart, the German spiritual leader, preached, 'Every creature is a word of God.'[33] So we journey with the book of scripture in one hand and the book of creation in the other.

We also remember that we are co-creators with God. We can learn through creative arts, whether information technology, flower arranging or poetry. We use and learn through all our senses. Through experiencing great art, observed former Czech president and playwright Vaclav Havel, we are opening up to 'the other' and to 'the beyond—to that which lies at the horizon of our being'.[34] This requires us to learn the biblical art of meditation. David Cole, in his book *The Mystic Path of Meditation*, writes that meditation 'is a state of concentrated attention… [It] is as normal and necessary as sleep… We extend our inner senses out to connect with God's Spirit around us.'[35]

Lifelong learning deepens through reflection on inspired people. 'Remember' is God's constant reminder to his people in the Old Testament: Remember what Abraham did, what lessons your forebears learned from Moses, and so on. 'Have you not heard?' asked Jesus. The church invites us—in the season of Advent, for example—to learn from prophets such as Isaiah and pioneers such as John the Baptist. All these can spur us to expand our thinking and living.

'Since we are surrounded by so great a cloud of witnesses…' says the letter writer to the Hebrews (12:1). The implication is that we should look at these Christians who have completed their course on earth and who witness to us, cheering us on in our race of faith. The cloud of witnesses is always growing. We may wish to draw desert fathers and mothers, Celtic saints, Spanish mystics or radical social workers into our field of studies.

Lifelong learning grows through reflection on experience. Self-knowledge lies at the heart of wisdom. Even mistakes can become learning opportunities as we invite the Holy Spirit to teach us. A time-honoured way of learning through experience is to reflect back on the day's events before we sleep. Some call this the 'examen'. Is there something for which to give thanks, something for which to say sorry, and some lesson we can learn? 'The unexamined life is not worth living,' said Socrates. 'I have learned,' said the apostle Paul, 'to be content... in any and all circumstances' (Philippians 4:11–12).

> *The Bible is... a conversation where various, sometimes harmonious and sometimes discordant, human voices contribute to the gradually growing picture of the character of Yahweh; fully revealed only in Jesus. But it is also a conversation that, rather than ending with the finalisation of the canon, continues beyond it, involving all those who give themselves to Christ's on-going redemptive movement.*[36]

This is a conversation, a habit, for every day of our lives. It is a fascinating dialogue because it is about the meaning of human life. Could multitudes of eavesdroppers, stressed and left empty by the world's mindless digital chatter, join this life-giving conversation?

REFLECTION

I imagine Aidan living alongside those he appointed as tutors in his monastic schools, laying out a curriculum that embraced study, prayer and soul friendship, how to learn from communal interactions, and how to integrate head learning with things of the heart and the hands.

Holistic learning has been lost to our society. Although Bede skips over such things, it seems clear that Irish monastics were often warriors who learned to integrate their physical and spiritual natures. Feats of endurance and daring in the inner life and in service to others marked them. The custom of standing in cold water, chanting praises and prayers, is one example. Cuthbert, an English product of Aidan's mission, like earlier Celtic Christians, practised it.

How may we develop such a holistic and integrative approach? Friends tell me of their rites of passage. They immerse themselves in water in order to get the depths of their being immersed in God. They see this as a pattern. They wrestle or roll in mud in order to become at home with the elements. They hit bales with sticks, in order to bring out things they are angry about. They run the gauntlet: after recalling negative things said about them by peers, which have stunted their lives, they tell these to the group, who yell them out while they run through the group and break the power of the negativities. They end their initiation weekends with chants of scripture so that their dysfunctional patterns are replaced with patterns of prayer and poise. This is in stark contrast to the absence of any rites of passage in our society, or to sick rites such as those practised by drunken rugby club members who strip naked and have sex with women for whom they have no respect. The Christian rites of initiation help men get in touch with their feminine and masculine dimensions, and to be tender and true.

I imagine Aidan seeing each person he met on his travels or at royal centres as children of God, with a capacity to learn less systematically, but just as really, from God in the Gospel stories and in everyday life. Ask, 'What is the God-shaped way of learning that best suits this person?' as you meet people today.

I imagine Aidan asking boys in his schools not to blame themselves or others for mistakes, but asking what they had learned from their experiences. 'If life is viewed as a maze, every mistake is an unnecessary detour and a waste of time. If life is a labyrinth, then every mistake is a part of the path and an indispensable master teacher.'[37] Before you sleep, reflect on lessons you have learned from things that have gone wrong or right during the day.

A little boy named Colton Burpo nearly died and apparently went to heaven. 'What did you do in heaven?' his father asked him. 'Homework,' he replied. 'Jesus was my teacher. Like school.

Jesus gave me work to do and that was my favourite part of heaven.'[38] What homework might Jesus wish to give you or those you care for?

Divine Mentor,
Teach us the habits of holy learning:
To know your ways
To explore your world
To learn from experience
To understand people
To manage time and talents
To draw on wellsprings of wisdom
Until we become a people of saints and scholars.

RELATIONSHIP TO THE EARTH

WE LOOK UPON CREATION AS A SACRAMENT THAT
REFLECTS THE GLORY OF GOD, AND SEEK TO MEET
GOD THROUGH CREATION, TO BLESS IT, AND TO
CELEBRATE IT.

COMMUNITY OF AIDAN AND HILDA WAY OF LIFE

Aidan's mission contrasts with mission models that take people
from the earthiness of their daily life into a church building
insulated from the elements. Aidan walked long distances
through the countryside, but the Christianity introduced by the
Roman mission under King Oswald's predecessor, Edwin, was an
indoors religion. Once they were baptised, people had to leave
their farmsteads and come to an unnatural, ornamented building
called a church. The Irish Christians left their indoor comforts to
go into the outdoors.

Although Aidan did encounter a less earthy and more Roman
approach during his lifetime, he could not have envisaged a
time when Christians would make no connection between the
Jesus who saves individuals from their sins and the Jesus who
sustains creation (John 1:2–3; Colossians 1:16–17). Too many
evangelistic Christians, who read the Bible through a lens formed
(unknown to them) by centuries of rationalism, industrialism,
individualism and consumerism, dismiss care for the earth as a

distraction from saving souls. Although Aidan could not have envisaged these developments, it was only 13 years after his death that the Synod of Whitby replaced the Irish way of being church, which was rooted in relationship, with a more regulatory way. H.J. Massingham, reflecting on that Synod, wrote, 'If the British Church had survived it is possible that the fissure between Christianity and nature, widening through the centuries, would not have cracked the unity of Western man's attitude to the universe.'[39]

The Celts generally experienced God in the elements. That is why they lit fires, praised God while standing in cold water, blessed the earth and allowed God to reveal himself to them in the wildness of wind. The Irish learned from the 'two books': the book of scripture and the book of nature. When Ciaran, founder of Clonmacnoise, was dying at a young age from the plague, he asked to be laid outside so that he could die with God under the canopy of his creation.

Aidan would have heard stories of Columba, the founder of his monastery at Iona. Columba bade a brother become guest-master for three days to a stray bird that had been swept off course by the wind and lay exhausted on the shore. Some scholars think that an early Irish nature poem, which includes the following lines, may have been written by Columba himself:

Delightful to me to be on an island hill, on the crest of a rock,
that I might often watch the quiet sea;
That I might watch the heavy waves above the bright water,
as they chant music to their Father everlastingly...
That I might watch the splendid flocks of birds over the well-
watered sea, that I might see its mighty whales, the greatest
wonder...
That I might bless the Lord who rules all things, heaven with its
splendid host, earth, ebb, and flood.

Many traditions tell of Columba's love for Derry and its oak woods. The local king gave Columba a plot of land in the oak grove near Derry, but like other Celtic monks before and since, Columba felt that it went against the grain to cut down trees. He would not build the church in the king's place of choice if it meant cutting down an oak. He left instructions that those who came after him should not cut down the trees and, if a tree fell in a gale, it was to be left for nine full days, out of respect, before being cut up and taken to the poor as firewood. Today, in Derry (Londonderry), people wear the oak leaf to commemorate Columba on 9 June. Here is part of a poem that Columba wrote about his beloved Derry of the Oaks:

I would give all for one little cell
In my beautiful Derry.
For its peace and for its purity...
For heaven's angels that come and go
Under every leaf of the oaks,
I love my little Derry.
My Derry, my fair oak grove,
My dear little cell and dwelling.

In the grounds of the monastery at Durrow, there was a tree that provided local people with a big supply of apples; however, the fruit tasted so bitter that the people complained. One autumn day, Columba went up to it and, seeing it laden with apples that were going to give more displeasure than pleasure to the people, he raised his hand and spoke to the tree: 'In the name of almighty God, bitter tree, may all your bitterness depart from you, and from now on may your apples be really sweet.' Columba's biographer commented, 'Wonderful to tell, more swiftly than words all the apples on that tree lost their bitterness and became wonderfully sweet'![40] Monks in the Columba tradition were familiar with the writings of Irenaeus, Athanasius and Basil. Irenaeus (d.202), the bishop of the large church of Celts at Lyons, taught that creation is an attribute of God's goodness. Through the resurrection of Christ, there would be a new heaven and earth (Revelation 21:1) and a new human body, and therefore 'neither the substance nor the essence of creation will be annihilated, although "the fashion" of the world passes away'.[41] In *Proof of the Apostolic Preaching*, Irenaeus offers a picture of the Son and the Spirit, the two hands of God, at the pinnacle of creation offering praise. His definition of 'creature' includes inbuilt direction towards God.[42]

Athanasius (d.373), the bishop of Alexandria, although twice exiled by Arian opponents, finally had his views on the Trinity adopted by the universal church at the Council of Nicea. A central issue for him was the question, 'Is God remote from creation or has God become one with creation through the uniting of God with human flesh in the incarnation of Christ?' Athanasius commended the churches in Celtic lands for never deviating from this trinitarian understanding.

Basil of Caesarea (d.379) wrote in Homily 5 of *Hexaemeron*, 'I want creation to penetrate you with so much admiration that wherever you go, the least plant may bring you the clear remembrance of the Creator.'[43] Columbanus of Bangor, who established many communities across Europe, taught his students in the first of his collected sermons, 'If you would know the Creator, get to know his creation' and 'If you trample on the earth, the earth will trample on you.'[44]

Caedmon, the cowherd at the Whitby monastery of Aidan's protégé Hilda, whom she empowered as a poet-singer, was inspired to compose songs about creation and 'the middle earth'. Bede translated his first poem from Caedmon's Anglo-Saxon into Latin. Among various translations into modern English is the following free translation, which perhaps best captures the spirit of the original:

Now must we hymn the Master of Heaven,
The might of the Maker, the deeds of the Father,

The thoughts of His heart.
The Lord Everlasting established the sun, the source of all wonder,
Creator, all holy,
He hung the high heavens,
a roof upreared o'er the children of men.
The King of mankind then created for mortals
the world in its beauty, the earth spread beneath them.
Green grew the grass there, dew dappled with daisies,
towered the tall trees bearing bright blossom.
Lovely and living, the life-giving light came
from Love everlasting, the Spirit, the Lord.

The theologian known to us as the Irish Augustine saw miracles in scripture and nature as interwoven. He saw the seven days of Genesis 1 as periods of time. He compares the virgin birth to creatures such as certain female fish who lay eggs without a male. Marina Smyth provides an exhaustive study of texts in her book *Understanding the Universe in Seventh-Century Ireland*.[45]

AT ONE WITH NATURE

Aidan's Irish Christians loved the stories of the fourth-century desert fathers and mothers of Egypt who left the second-hand faith of comfortable cities to live alone with God in deserted places, there to engage in spiritual warfare with the devil. The Irish kept three seasons of Lent, not one, so that they could make vigil in wild places. That is why one of Aidan's first acts amid his busy schedule was to retire to the Inner Farne Isle to be alone with God among the birds and the elements. It is also why Aidan taught that people could encounter God among the elements, even in a wild storm at sea.

One of Aidan's most esteemed priests, Utta, Abbot of Gateshead, was asked to supervise the escort of Kent's Princess Eanfled, who was to become King Oswy's queen, by sea up to Bamburgh. This was a delicate and dangerous undertaking so he discussed it with Aidan and begged his prayers for everyone involved. The prophetic Aidan warned that they would indeed meet a storm. He blessed them and commended them to the Lord and at the same time gave them a phial of oil, saying, 'When you meet the storm, be mindful to pour this oil on to the sea and the wind will cease immediately; you will then have calm, pleasant weather to accompany you all the way home.' All these things happened as Aidan had said. At first the sailors tried to ride out the storm at anchor, but to no avail. The boat filled with water and they feared death would overtake them. It was only then that Utta remembered the phial of oil. He poured this oil on the troubled waters, which at once became calm. This is the origin of the phrase that has passed into the English language: 'to pour oil on troubled waters' (*EH* 3.15).

This is reminiscent of the Gospels' story of Jesus and his disciples in a storm-tossed boat on Lake Galilee, where the disciples feared for their lives (Matthew 8:23–27). When Jesus rebuked the wind and the waves, they obeyed him. That story reveals the intimate connection between God the Creator and God in creation.

HEALING THE LAND

Aidan and the Irish missionaries were not naively romantic about nature. Aidan believed that land needed to be healed. He taught his flock to fast and pray for 40 days on any piece of land that was to have buildings erected for a faith community; it was important to engage in spiritual battle in order to cleanse it of bad influences.

One of four English lads who were steeped in Aidan's teachings at Lindisfarne's school was Cedd. After Aidan's death, he was sent as missionary bishop to the East Saxons, in the area that is today's Essex. He often made retreat back in Northumbria. Oswy's regent in Deira, whom Bede names as Oidilwald, urged Cedd to build a monastic place of prayer on some land where he, Oidilwald, might go to pray to the Lord and hear the word, and where he might be buried, for he believed that he should receive benefit from the daily prayers of those who served the Lord in that place. Cedd's brother Caelin administered the word and sacraments to the regent and his household. Cedd chose a place among steep and distant mountains, which looked more like lurking-places for robbers and dens of wild beasts than civilised human dwelling places. But, observed Bede, quoting the prophecy of Isaiah, 'In the habitation of dragons, where each lay, might be grass with reeds and rushes'—that is, that the fruits of good works should spring up, where before beasts were wont to dwell, or people to live after the manner of beasts.

First, however, Cedd desired to cleanse the place from the stain of former crimes, by prayer and fasting. He asked the regent's permission to stay in prayer there throughout the 40 days of Lent, not eating until evening. He told the regent that this was the custom they had learned from Aidan. While there were ten days remaining in Lent, Cedd was summoned back by the East Saxons' king. In order not to undermine the '40 days rule', he persuaded his brother and priest, Cynebill, to take his place. Cynebill readily agreed and, upon completing the vigil, he built the monastery of prayer in that place, which we know as Lastingham, based on the practices of Aidan's Lindisfarne where he, too, had been trained (*EH* 3.23).

Praying over land for 40 days is part of the wider call to heal the land. Genesis 4 recounts how the land became sterile as a result of the misdeeds that humans such as Cain committed upon it. There is a law of cause and effect. This, too, is part of mission.

Russ Parker writes in his book *Healing Wounded History: Reconciling peoples and healing places*:

> *Throughout scripture we are taught that there is a direct con-*
> *nection between human story and the land or ground on*

which this story occurs. In challenging the people of God to seek forgiveness and healing of their sins, God promises to forgive those sins and, much more, to heal their land. One of the recurring threads in the prayers of consecration for this first temple is the connection between forgiveness of the sins of the nation and a restored connection with the land. For example, defeat in a war at the hands of an enemy (2 Chronicles 6:24–25) is thought to be the result of national sin, and returning to the land is a consequence of confession and repentance. When the nation is not living the community lifestyle which reflects God's principles the land suffers with drought, but forgiveness brings rain and a restored community life (2 Chronicles 6:26–27). There are over 2500 references to land in the Old Testament and over 250 in the New.[46]

A succession of biblical leaders cry to God to heal or restore their land (for example, Solomon in 2 Chronicles 6:14–40, as well as Ezra and Nehemiah), and they ask forgiveness as representatives of their abusive people. Prophets visualise times when humans and creation will be in harmony (for example, Isaiah 11:1–9). The Bible climaxes with John's vision of a unified heaven and earth (Revelation 21:1–5).

Three Australian siblings who inherited bush land at Buderim from forebears who were part of the 'land-grab' are an example of what landowners can do. They legally covenanted part of their land in perpetuity through the Beaulah Community Ltd Trust, which states:

We acknowledge the traditional custodians of the land and their care for it for thousands of years. We remember that they were forced unjustly from their land. We bear witness to the pain of that dispossession. Open to the Spirit, who was always present here, we resolve to appreciate the beauty of the land, protect its resources, remember its history and honour its traditional custodians.

Two of the three siblings—Heather Johnston, who has taken vows with the Community of Aidan and Hilda, and her sister Susie— have painstakingly researched the true history of the land-grabs and massacres. Indigenous peoples have returned to their land for the first time for more than 100 years. The following prayer has been used at one of their regular acts of prayer and penitence:

Big Heart of God, from you came the mountains and deserts, red and brown soil, water holes, creatures—and human beings. You gave us beautiful bodies, and you want us to have even more beautiful characters and to grow in wisdom. You desire us to be different tribes united in one fellowship like a rainbow.

We are sorry that we who settled here thousands of years ago, and we who settled here hundreds of years ago, have, in different ways, failed to reflect your beautiful nature in our lives. We have told lies or we have failed to listen to other people. We have been greedy or we have drowned our sorrows in wrong things. We have been proud or thoughtless or spiteful.

We know that your Son Jesus was not like that. Jesus was always tender, true and trusting in you, even when he was being killed. In his spirit he was as free as the birds that fly high and as the gentle winds. We know that Jesus lives in you, and we invite you to live in us.

Forgive us for bad things in the past. Scatter seeds of hope in our souls. Warm and water these seeds until they grow strong.[47]

STEWARDS OF THE LAND

Irish monastic communities typically earned their keep through the land that they stewarded. In Ireland these were called 'Termon' lands, probably because *termini*, pillar stones or crosses, were set up to mark their boundaries. Within these boundaries, those who sought sanctuary were safe, and no landowner or chief could levy taxes.

These lands were tilled or tended by monks. Some monasteries had the *manaig*—quarters where married people in vows could work the land. Aidan and his successors, often through their sponsoring king, were given substantial lands to farm.

In the Old Testament, the land ultimately belongs to God, and humans are but stewards of it. Leviticus 25:23 states, 'The land shall not be sold in perpetuity, for the land is mine; with me you are but aliens and tenants.' First Nation peoples understand this. Aidan understood it. He exemplifies Jesus' beatitude, 'Blessed are the meek, for they will inherit the earth' (Matthew 5:5). Aidan challenges us to root out possessiveness.

In scripture, the land awakens us to our calling. 'The land connects me,' says an Aboriginal man in Victoria, Australia. But Christians in the techno and industrial deserts of the West, who have been reared in a perversion of scriptural teaching that privatises salvation and suggests it has nothing to do with the land, do not know this.

In the early myths of the Celts, the god of the tribe mates with the goddess of the earth. The early church, secure in its Jewish roots, understood this divine connection with the earth. God named the first man *Adamah*, meaning 'Earth' (Genesis 2:7). Mr Earth's first act was to name, and thereby bless, each of earth's creatures (v. 20). In other words, humans contain within themselves the whole earth. When funerals are conducted, the final liturgy declares, 'We therefore commit this body to the ground; earth to earth, ashes to ashes, dust to dust.' These words are taken from Genesis 3:19: 'By the sweat of your brow you will eat your food until you return to the ground, since from it you were taken; for dust you are and to dust you will return.'

The biblical scholar Walter Brueggemann explores the theology of land. He writes of the sabbath principle, 'Sabbath, in the first instance, is not about worship. It is about work stoppage. It is about withdrawal from the anxiety system of Pharaoh, the refusal to let one's life be defined by production and consumption and the endless pursuit of private well-being.'[48]

Columba's monastic family observed the sabbath rest. Columba thought that Saturday should not be a typical work day, and we may presume that Aidan taught the same among the English. This is a challenge to Christians who tie mission to a campaign to restore Old Testament physical boundaries to the present state of Israel. Possessiveness, let alone conquest by force, has no part in Christ-like mission.

After centuries when the church has been thought to belittle the earth, we have a pope who calls us to cherish it. Pope Francis begins his Encyclical letter *Laudato Si: On Care for Our Common Home*:

'Praise be to you, my Lord.' In the words of this beautiful canticle, Saint Francis of Assisi reminds us that our common home is like a sister with whom we share our life and a beautiful mother who opens her arms to embrace us. This sister now cries out to us because of the harm we have inflicted on her by our irresponsible use and abuse of the goods with which God has endowed her. We have come to see ourselves as her lords and masters, entitled to plunder her at will. The violence present in our hearts, wounded by sin, is also reflected in the symptoms of sickness evident in the soil, in the water, in the air and in all forms of life. This is why the earth herself, burdened and laid waste, is among the most abandoned and maltreated of our poor; she 'groans in travail' (Romans 8:22). We have forgotten that we ourselves are dust of the earth (cf. Genesis 2:7); our very bodies are made up of her elements, we breathe her air and we receive life and refreshment from her waters. Nothing in this world is indifferent to us.[49]

It has taken over 14 centuries for the church to begin to address 'the fissure' referred to by H.J. Massingham. Even now, although the Anglican Communion identifies 'The integrity of creation' as its Fifth Mark of Mission and asks members to fast for climate change on the first day of every month, missional movements such as Fresh Expressions of Church make no mention of ecology in their criteria. However, a number of mission-orientated movements are very aware of the environment and of climate change as a key ethical issue.

Forest Church is one example. This fresh expression of church, drawing on much older traditions, when sacred places and practices were outside, also draws upon contemporary research that highlights the benefits of spending time with nature in wild places. Forest Church isn't just normal church happening outside: 'Instead it attempts to participate with creation. And it isn't just a fellowship group doing an outside activity; we aim to learn, worship, meditate, pray and practise with the trees, at the spring, along the shore.'[50]

Many churches are now creating community gardens. This is of particular use for the inner city where land is scarce. People have increasingly become aware of their consumer nature and are making simple steps towards getting in touch with being producers again. Churches with too small a curtilage to use as a reliable food source can still use it to make a prophetic statement. Churches also use such spaces for labyrinths or nature trails with meditation posts.

EARTHY PARABLES

In William Herzog's book *Parables as Subversive Speech*, he shatters the contemporary understanding that parables are earthly stories with heavenly meanings. Herzog declares that, if read properly, the parables of Jesus are actually 'earthy' stories with 'heavy' meanings. These stories depict everyday life for peasants, whom Jesus empowered by allowing them to understand the world on their own terms. Ruthless masters and absentee landowners are not code for God, but are just that—rich people, exploiting the poor who are trying to scrape together a subsistence living from the earth.[51]

Ched Myers retells the parable of the talents (Matthew

25:14–30) through the eyes of the first-century agrarian peasant rather than through the late capitalist lens that we tend to use. In contemporary reading we often neglect the fact that a 'talent' is a large unit of currency. We spiritualise it as the 'skills' that God has given us. This brings major issues, for the 'good' slaves who put the talents to work and made a massive return on their investment would have had to be unscrupulous. The Master, who is described as a 'hard' man who reaps where he does not sow (and whom we usually equate to God), is very angry with the third slave who buries his talent, saying that the slave could at least have gained interest on it (usury, which is frowned upon in the scriptures). This slave is banished from the household because he hasn't followed the system. Myers says that this is like an 'agrarian joke'. The slave buried the money but it did no good. It wasn't organic. It did not grow.[52]

CONNECTION TO THE EARTH

In our book *Celtic Spirituality in the Australian Landscape*, Brent explains about the connection to land. His interest in Celtic Christianity began when he moved into an intentional Christian community in Melbourne where they studied George MacLeod's vision for the Iona community. One of the exercises they undertook as a community was to trace their genealogy to obtain a greater understanding of who they were. Brent discovered that he was a third-generation Aussie and Anglo-Celtic through and through.

Tracing the footsteps of his ancestors intrigued him and he made a pilgrimage around the UK, exploring many significant holy sites. When he arrived back in Australia after only several weeks away, he felt like an exile in his own country. The wide brown land didn't quite seem right; he was longing for the rolling green hills. He read David Tacey's book *ReEnchantment*, which pointed out that the power of the land and the influence of

Aboriginal culture are activating primordial levels of the Euro-Australian psyche, stirring its deeper layers. Tacey believes that a version of ancient Celtic spirituality is being awakened and stirred to new life in Australia. We can see many signs of this in Australian folk culture, where the attempt to 'grow down' into Australian soil has the effect of revitalising Celtic roots, giving rise to a kind of Celtic revival.[53]

Brent learned, through relationships with Aboriginal people, that they find identity in the connection with their land. One Aboriginal man explained that he was using drugs to cover the pain of his dislocation from his 'mob' up in rural Australia.

Brent never really knew what connection to land meant until he went to the UK and started walking on the land of his ancestors and hearing the stories of 'his' people. Anglos may not ever understand or feel the depth of connection to land that indigenous Australians do, but this is an important insight into the way indigenous cultures are at one with their land and place.

Irish Christians had an awareness of God's presence in creation, a practice of relating prayer and work to creation's rhythms, a closeness to the earth, the elements and animals magnified in the lives of various saints, and an empathy expressed in worship, poetry and art. In the monasteries of Aidan, work and prayer are two sides of the same coin. There is a synergy between the Spirit, the work of human hands and the rest of creation.

REFLECTION

I imagine Aidan coming to a place and leaving an impression wherever he stopped. I imagine him relaxing into the earth, aware that he came from earth and would pass into the earth. He lingered long and his presence somehow seeped into the landscape.

'Landscape has a secret and silent memory, a narrative of presence where nothing is ever lost or forgotten.'[54] What holy or wholesome presences do you sense in the area where you live or work?

Aidan did not put up paltry, artificial constructs that distanced him from earth. 'Holy people draw to themselves earthy things,' wrote Hildegard of Bingen.[55] What earthy things are being drawn to you?

There are two approaches to mission: that of the victor and that of the vulnerable. Aidan's approach was that of the vulnerable. The vulnerable are like humus: discarded in the ground, it forms nutrients in which things may grow. 'Only when the last tree has died and the last river has been poisoned and the last fish has been caught will we realise that we cannot eat money,' said a 19th-century Cree Indian. In what ways does your mission work reflect the victor and in what ways does it reflect humus?

'When we lose our map, our real knowledge of the path begins. It's humbling because we're forced to touch the Earth itself,' says Mark Nepo.[56] As we love the earth and the animals, people will love God. How do you see that happening?

How may these practices and awarenesses be embedded in our personal and common life?

A PRAYER OF THE FOUR ELEMENTS

Aidan's prayer turned round the winds: may we be borne along by your winds.

Aidan's blessed oil calmed troubled waters: may our souls be lapped by your gentle waters.

Aidan soaked a place in prayer for 40 days: may the earth remind us to live on it with prayer.

Aidan's name means 'fire': kindle in us the fires of your love.

VILLAGES OF GOD: MODELLING GOD'S KINGDOM ON EARTH

THE CELTIC MONASTERIES WERE 'COLONIES OF HEAVEN' PLANTED ON EARTH AS A SIGN AND HARBINGER OF THE KINGDOM THAT WAS YET TO COME.

IAN BRADLEY

The 1979 meeting of the Latin American Catholic bishops at Puebla taught that 'evangelisation is a call to participation in trinitarian community' (no. 218). Leonardo Boff comments, 'This applies in a very basic way to the church as institution. Yet, we must recognise that the spirit of communion—and hence the trinitarian root of the church—has been best preserved in religious life and in popular Christianity where power has been shared.'[57] Churches in the form they have taken in recent centuries face life-threatening problems. Attendance has plunged. Instead of being the community that transforms the wider community, the church is seen as a monocultural refuge for a minority. It is not surprising that many people inside and outside these churches look for something more effective. However, this 'something' needs to be more holistic than are some current responses, which I have listed below as 'Institutional', 'Attractional', 'Do it yourself' and 'Mission only' models.

INSTITUTIONAL

The institutional model pays a pastor to keep members happy, but they cease to be happy if the pastor has to relate to growing numbers of people, whether in one larger or several smaller churches. When decline becomes sufficiently serious, the institutional model pays an ordained manager to oversee an increased number of amalgamated parishes. The first problem is that bishops or their equivalents deal with shrinkage by management rather than by transformation. A priest in a declining Church of England diocese tells me:

> My diocese 'sells' the doubling of posts by telling the priests they won't be expected to do all the things they previously did. But the people have not been prepared, and are unwilling to do duties they think the priest is paid to do. So the priest becomes frustrated and burned out. It would be better if the diocese appointed an interim priest for a year or two, to prepare the church members both for changes in their duties and for a transformed understanding of the nature of church and of their calling to a life rooted in prayer, reflection and outreach.

In the Diocese of London, decline has stalled. This is largely due to immigration but may also be because London's bishops tend to support fresh approaches born in the hearts of their clergy. Elsewhere, decline is widespread, yet I know of at least one diocese that still puts nearly all its eggs into the basket of the parish system. While Pope Francis calls for churches to be the spiritual home of all, too many parish churches become ghettos for those who wish to cling on to an archaic, monocultural ritual.

This appraisal focuses on a widespread weakness in institutional churches, but we should remember that wherever pastors follow Jesus' words in John 5:19 ('The Son can do nothing on his own, but only what he sees the Father doing'), there is the kingdom of God.

ATTRACTIONAL

The attractional model finds out what spiritual consumers want and gives it to them. This approach is well-known in politics. Political leaders employ focus groups. The leaders then produce policies or programmes that, at the least, are dressed up in the language used by focus group participants. This has famously been the approach of Willow Creek Church, USA. However, this congregation of some 30,000 discovered after several years that as many people left by the back door as entered by the front door. The leaders concluded that programmes without the inculcation of self-sustaining disciplines lacked viability.

The attractional model, removed from a consumerist culture, appears in the Old Testament. Jerusalem, set on a hill, attracted pilgrims from throughout the country. Its life revolved around the vast and many-splendoured hub of the temple, a seven-days-a-week hive of activity and prayer. The vision was that every facet of the city should be in harmony:

> *Jerusalem, well-built city,*
> *built as a place for worship!*
> *The city to which the tribes ascend,*
> *all God's tribes go up to worship,*
> *to give thanks to the name of God—*
> *this is what it means to be Israel.*
> *Thrones for righteous judgment*
> *are set there, famous David-thrones.*
> *Pray for Jerusalem's peace!*
> *Prosperity to all you Jerusalem-lovers!'*
> *(Psalm 122:3–6, THE MESSAGE).*

Jerusalem, like any place that attracts people, put the means before the end. It put products before God and so, once again, it was dispersed.

DO IT YOURSELF

A major problem is that Protestantism has degenerated into denominationalism. It is said there are 400,000 denominations, irredeemably fragmented. This is in part because so many of them prioritise points of view as the determining factor. When people agree, they gather: when they disagree, they split. In a family, though, people stay together not because they agree but because they are family. So it is meant to be with the church.

One example of the 'Do it yourself' approach is Organic Church. It claims—as do many sects, such as the Mormons—that the right model is to disregard existing branches of the worldwide Christian church and start from scratch, by basing everything only on Jesus and his love. 'We mean a non-traditional church that is birthed naturally or organically from the Life of Christ in His disciples instead of one constructed by human institutional systems and kept together by various programs and rituals,' it says. So it calls on Christians to leave 'the religious system'. Since the foundation is love (John 13:34–35), this way of being church is best expressed in a family setting.

The glaring error is that all the sins we see in the church as an institution are also in ourselves.[58] I learned this when, in an almost unique experiment, I was entrusted to establish 'one family of Christians for one neighbourhood' at Bowthorpe, Norwich. True, I was invited by the denominations, but we were given two years to experiment in the light of the new neighbourhood's unique culture before their sponsoring body formalised our emerging structures. I once quipped, 'We thought we started this project free from the church baggage of centuries; but we have created more of our own baggage in two years than they have in two centuries.'

A new church that does not work on its members' 'shadow' (the unacceptable parts of ourselves that we'd rather not acknowledge) does not ring true. The 'shadow' is a modern term. The desert tradition within Christianity, the tradition of ceaseless warfare against the inner demons, is a biblical necessity. A sympathetic critic advised people from such an expression of church: read the Bible from the heart as well as from the head; use all ways of praying; and, since Moses, Elijah, Jesus and Paul needed to spend time in a desert, follow their example.

MISSION ONLY

We referred to the missional model of church in the first chapter, and to its commendable attempt to break out of familiar comfort zones and reach people in new spheres with the gospel of Christ. However, this model, too, needs to be lovingly challenged. There is no intrinsic value in mission per se. The worth of a mission is determined by its values, not its productivity. The problem with a 'Mission only' model is that it puts the part before the whole. It makes an idol of mission. Legitimate questions we should ask are: 'By what authority do you engage in the work? How well do you relate to the full values and scope of the kingdom of God? How well do you relate to other parts of Christ's body in the area or context of your work? How do you ensure that you see, act and live as God desires?'

AIDAN'S MODEL

Aidan's vision of church could be described as God-shaped hub communities that have a heart for God, others and society.

Aidan established his first monastic hub on the tidal island of Lindisfarne. Perhaps he chose this place because it enabled a daily rhythm of seclusion when the tide was high and connection to the mainland when the tide was low. It was near enough to Bamburgh to receive royal protection if it was attacked, but far enough away not to be taken over by the affairs of the world. Perhaps Aidan had heard that, until the Saxons invaded, this island was known to the Britons as Medcaut, meaning 'healing'. Richard Coates has proposed 'Medicata' (British Celtic influenced by Latin) as the etymon for Medcaut or Medcaud (compare the modern Welsh *meddyg*, meaning 'doctor'). The expected sense would be the passive 'healed'.[59]

King Oswald sent staff with practical skills to help the brothers establish a very simple monastic settlement. The church was made of oak planks with a thatched roof. Cells were erected for the brothers and for students in the planned school for English boys. Sapling branches were woven together and fixed to upright poles; the gaps were sealed with mud.

Because Lindisfarne was so effective, a network of such communities developed. Like Lindisfarne, in addition to the simple wooden huts for the brothers, students and workers, each community generally had a school, a library and a scriptorium, a kitchen and guest quarters. There were fields where sheep, goats and cows were tended and where barley or wheat was grown. Those near water had boats and fishing facilities. Spinning, weaving and woodwork went on. Sometimes there were social occasions with music and poetry, and times for feasting as well as for fasting.

Visitors soon began to come. The brothers were taught to receive the visitors as if they were Christ. Students were taught not only to give to others but to give of themselves. On Sundays the people flocked to the monasteries, not primarily to feed their bodies but to hear the word of God. Great attention was paid to the brothers' exhortations.

Aidan would have known of Ireland's tribal network of seven-days-a-week faith communities. Each had its local character, but there were common features. In his book *Colonies of Heaven: Celtic models for today's church*, Ian Bradley points out that early Christians in Ireland often lived together in monastic colonies, which were the hubs of tribal life, lived in from the perspective of eternity. Teams of people (some ordained) lived in community and went out among the people, meeting their pastoral needs. These hubs supported many types of ministry—solitary hermits, married monks, professed monks and nuns, lay brothers and sisters, regular and secular clergy, ordained and non-ordained. They were joined by pilgrims, penitents and other guests, and they were highly committed to both the active and the contemplative life. Bradley comments that the monasteries served in many ways, as 'hospital, hotel, school, university, arts workshop, open prison and reformatory, night shelter and drop-in day centre as well as church, retreat house, mission station and place of prayer and spiritual healing'.[60] They were open and accessible to visitors coming and going. Both the active and the contemplative roles made the monastery a colony of heaven, rooted in the world, serving it and intimately involved in its affairs, yet the embodiment of radically otherworldly values.

Iona, since it was an island, was less open to the world than, say, St Brigid's Kildare, to which thousands constantly thronged. Iona was somewhat more austere. According to the archaeological evidence and references in contemporary literature pieced together by Thomas Owen Clancy and Gilbert Markus in *Iona: The earliest poetry of a Celtic monastery*, the monastery was surrounded by a vallum, open to the sea on the eastern side and bounded with walls of dry-built stone 300–400 metres north to south.[61] Within this boundary were the monks' dwellings, workshops and church, all built of wood. The church was large enough to hold the entire community at prayer. It had a side chapel. Monks would go to pray communally up to eight times every 24 hours, and sometimes alone. A large communal building was used for teaching, study, reading and writing. It is not clear whether this building was also used as a kitchen and refectory. Some monks had individual cells, and others, presumably the younger ones, shared a dormitory. Columba had a small cell on a rocky outcrop where he would work each day, transcribing his beloved psalms. Such Celtic monasteries resembled the groups of hermits' cells in the east more than the isolation of later enclosed Benedictine monasteries.

Outside the vallum, on the western side of the island, was a building where guests were fed and cared for. Farming activities also took place outside the vallum. It seems they had cattle, red deer, sheep, pigs, horses, otters, grey seal, whale and roe deer, although the eating of horse flesh was forbidden. Adomnan's *Life of Columba* contains references to the cultivation of barley, milking of cows, slaughter of beef cattle and fishing in the River Shiel. All this, and timber felling, required barns for storage, carts and boats for transport, enclosures for animals, and workshops for the making of tools such as axes, knives, lathes and drills, and for pottery and leather-working. The Irish monasteries were centres of labour and were self-supporting.

Adomnan alludes several times to the work of writing and copying carried on by the abbot and his monks, which at Kells, Iona and Lindisfarne produced masterpieces of Celtic art. Life on Iona was not all work; it was pervaded by 'heavenly vision'. It was widely acknowledged in Columban monasteries that some scriptures were difficult to interpret. Adomnan wrote of Columba, 'Everything that in the sacred scriptures is dark and most difficult became more plain' as a result of mystical experience.[62]

These Irish monasteries were led by a spiritual parent named an *abba*, or abbot. Even the bishop, who was part of the monastic family, accepted the abbot's authority. Bede reports that this was the practice on Iona (*EH* 3.4). It was a tribal family, not a diocesan system.

A. Hamilton Thompson writes in his chapter on 'Northumbrian monasticism' in *Bede: His life, times, and writings*:

> It is from the self-supporting monastery, dependent upon the labour of its inmates, at once a place of prayer and contemplation, an active centre of labour, a training-school for the religious life, and a home of sacred learning, that ideal pictures of medieval monastic life have been frequently drawn; and although in later times this ideal was partially revived... its fullest realisation was

in these Celtic monasteries founded in the midst of a turbulent and uncivilised society and affording a sanctuary to the oppressed and an example of peaceful and concentrated activity to their whole neighbourhood. But with the monastic life was combined the work of evangelisation... distant from home.[63]

The monasteries that Aidan established in Britain were seven-days-a-week, multifaceted communities of work, prayer, learning, hospitality and mission, like those in Ireland but with one major difference. The Irish monastic settlements were harnessed to the tribal system. The abbot became the chief of the tribe's church. The abbot's successor (the *coarb*, literally the 'heir') could usually claim lineal descent of some sort from the founder. The native name for the monastic community was *muintir*, which in Latin is translated as *familia*—family. At Iona, Columba and 13 of his successors were descended from an Irish chief named Conall Gulban.

The monastic family consisted of brothers (*fratres*), seniors (*seniores*, those of tried and tested devotion), the stronger ones who did manual work (*operarii fraters*) and those under instruction—juniors, alumni and members of families within the settlement. Officers of the monastery included the abbot (the spiritual parent), the prior (the administrator), the bishop (who ordained and confirmed), the scribe (an expert scholar and inscriber) and the *erinach* (the lay manager of the lands). Pilgrims, penitents and guests of various kinds were also present.

Abbots were usually related to the founder because they inherited the lands that went with the monastery. That custom was not extended to the English, because the leader was a bishop and did not own land. The leadership of English monasteries was not based on tribal hierarchy. Aidan's episcopal see was at Lindisfarne but he was often elsewhere. He appointed an abbot who was under his authority. Nevertheless, there was a family feel. Four brothers came to Lindisfarne together (*EH* 4.27).

Leicester University archaeologists have delineated what they believe to be the bounds of the original monastic rath (enclosure) at Lindisfarne. It mirrors in size and shape the Ionan model.[64] On the Sunday nearest St Aidan's Day, 31 August, the parish church walks these bounds and sometimes a bishop blesses the island from the hill known locally as the heugh. The bounds are from the present church along the road by the shore (Fiddlers Green), turning right down Marygate, and right again along what was the original harbour shore (now the slope in Sanctuary Field), up to the heugh and back to the church.

Aidan's first monasteries were frugal. They had no invested money. The wealthy people did not resort to these monasteries, except to pray and hear the word of God. The king himself, when occasion required, came only with five or six servants and, having performed his devotions in the church, departed. If they happened to take a repast there, they were satisfied with the plain daily food of the brothers and required no more, for the whole care of the teachers was to serve God, not the world—to feed the soul and not the belly. Lindisfarne was a missionary monastery. Production of Gospels and psalms for use in evangelisation was a priority, but learning was important, too.

We do not know the names of all the monastic communities planted in England directly or indirectly through the influence of Aidan's mission, but they included Bradwell, Coldingham, Gateshead, Hartlepool, Hackness, Lastingham, Lichfield, Lindisfarne, Melrose, Repton, Tilbury, Whitby and perhaps St Bees in Cumbria. This list excludes communities such as Ripon, which for a time had oversight from Aidan's disciples, and Gilling, whose first abbot was King Oswin's relative. His successor, Cynefrid, studied the scriptures in Ireland and entrusted the monastery to Tunberct. Tunberct then mentored Cynefrid's brother Ceolfrid in monastic discipline.

Following an outbreak of plague, Tunberct, Cynefrid and other surviving monks joined the community at Ripon. Thus, even after Wilfrid had taken charge of Ripon, it retained an Irish presence. It was from Ripon that Willibrord, the apostle of Frisia, went to improve his learning in Ireland. Ceolfrid left Ripon to join Benedict Biscop at Wearmouth. Tunberct presumably remained at Ripon until he was consecrated bishop of Hexham by Theodore. Etheldreda, who never consummated her marriage to Oswy's son Ecgfrid, was trained in the monastic life at Coldingham before founding the monastery at Ely. A woman's monastery at Watton, in the East Riding of Yorkshire, is mentioned in a miracle story (recorded by Bede) of Bishop John of Beverley, one of Hilda's students.

Bede is contradictory. On the one hand, he espoused the system of churches under bishops with diocesan boundaries; on the other hand, he deplored the superficial spirituality of these churches in his time, and thought it was through the monasteries that the best of the church could most fruitfully be developed. F.E. Warren claims that 'in most histories the missionary work of St Augustine is grossly exaggerated and the important missionary and educational work of the Irish monks is either completely ignored or accorded an amount of space utterly out of proportion to its importance'.[65]

THEN AND NOW

At first sight there is no connection between the context of today's global village and the world of Aidan's monastic villages. However, in a lecture at St Andrew's University entitled 'Does the future have a church?' I made the following points. They have become a kind of mantra and I repeat them here:

- A 24-hour society calls for seven-days-a-week faith communities.
- A café society calls for churches that are eating places.
- A travelling society calls for churches that provide accommodation.

- A stressed society calls for churches that nurture retreats and meditation.
- A multi-choice society calls for churches that have a choice of styles and facilities.
- A fragmented society calls for holistic models and whole-life discipling.
- An eco-threatened society calls for more locally sustainable communities that have roots in the soil.

Ian Bradley thinks that today's church might seek to emulate this functioning of different ministries from a communal base. He wishes that the new-style *monasteria* would be ecumenical and non-denominational. He envisions 'modern *monasteria* with clusters of cells and satellite groups based around central or minster churches... promot[ing] an integrative and unifying ecclesiology at a time when so many current pressures tend towards splitting and fragmentation'.[66]

Moreover, globalisation is, paradoxically, bringing a revival of the city. A group met in my garden that included Graham Ward, Professor of Contextual Theology and Ethics at Manchester University. In his book *Cities of God*, he notes the city states that made up medieval Europe, and says that contemporary social atomism has led to cities of desires fed by capitalism's ephemeral vanities. There is both an emptiness and a hunger for something more real and lasting that might inspire these cities to something greater. Bruce Katz, Vice President and Director of the Metropolitan Policy Program at The Brookings Institution, has suggested that in 2016 'nations may govern but cities rule'. There are signs that churches are responding to this re-emergence of the city. The focus of the 2000-member Central Church Edinburgh (a Baptist and transdenominational church that attracts people from a wider spectrum to its leadership team) is to bring in the kingdom of God to the whole city.[67] It seems to me that, although selfish individualism reigns, longing for community and ultimate significance also grows.

With the advent of advanced technology and freedom of movement, endless forces now move and coalesce. The Holy Spirit accompanies all these external forces and the movements within people's hearts. Globalisation and mass communication enable the rise of what has been termed 'liquid church'. This fluidity enables separate entities to flow together, the parts to coalesce with a greater whole, and this coalescing requires intelligent and coordinated responses from Christians. That is why Graham Ward foresees cities of God emerging through the coalescing of a kaleidoscope of spiritual dynamics.

We must plant expressions of Christ in the places to which people gravitate today—in blogging and eating places, in pilgrim and study places, in natural and social places. We must 'move to the edge of empire' where there is neither dispossession nor domination, neither labelling nor hidden agendas. In doing this, we must not collude with those who wish to replace Christendom with anarchy, of the sort God condemned in the period of the Old Testament judges, when 'everyone did what was right in their own eyes', without regard to the common good or the call to build community (Judges 21:25).

The mushrooming of Christian projects, culture-friendly church plants, missional groups and networks, alongside the decline in the 'one-shape-fits-all' type of church, makes possible patterns that are more flexible than the old. In the spirit of Jeremiah, who called God's people to seek the good of the city (Jeremiah 29:7), some Christians envision patterns emerging that cohere around some common values, facilities and rhythms. I use the term 'villages of God' for these patterns. (I have heard some Americans use the term 'mall'.)

Why the term 'village'? In large cities, shopping centres and airports throughout the world, you now see signs such as 'the village', 'youth city', 'waterside village', 'sky city', 'Mediterranean village' and 'sports village'. Why? Because the marketeers know that people want something more than the sale of products: they want the feeling that they can be at home and in community. Of course, this is mostly a sham; perhaps it will give 'village' such a bad name that we will have to invent a new name—but for now it will do.

HOW VILLAGES OF GOD MAY EMERGE

Villages of God start where people are. In the future, a few may be designed from scratch, as Quakers once designed model villages such as Bournville. Some can grow piecemeal, as a core group responds to the Holy Spirit at work in their area. A virtual village may evolve even in rural areas when isolated churches and projects link up. The primary basis for a village of God is a hub church or monastic community with varied facilities that develops partnerships with service providers around it. In Russia, monastic kremlins of over a mile in circumference are being rebuilt and repopulated in town centres. Leo Tolstoy thought that the beehive was a model for human community.

VILLAGES OF GOD DESIGNED FOR NEW AREAS

As we look to the future, we should be alert to possibilities to build new settlements whose design reflects principles of the village of God. Enlightened planners have experimented to find the shapes that bring most well-being to cities and neighbourhoods. For example, the five- or eight-point star was used at one time. This provided for a hub, with facilities and housing within each of the star points and green spaces in between, but the advent of the car undermined its good intentions.[68]

Richard Summers, a past President of the Royal Town Planning Institute, the UK's leading planning body for spatial, sustainable and inclusive planning and the largest planning institute in Europe, attended a retreat I led, which explored villages of God. He emailed:

The 'Celtic Christian village' puts a cultural driving force behind 'central place theory' and the traditional ideas of 'rural settlement patterns' in planning... I hope the evolution of planning theory and practice from Christaller to the NPPF will cast further light on your teaching and perhaps lead to some further collaboration on the role of Celtic Christianity in the early development of human settlement that lay the foundations for the complex urban and rural systems we live within today.[69]

An example of a purpose-designed village is Poatina in Tasmania, sponsored by Fusion Australia, a Christian youth and community organisation. It comprises a three-star motel, mountain view restaurant, mountain cottages, backpackers' hostel, 54 brick-veneer houses, community hall, offices, general store, gift shop, service station, post office, metal fabrication workshop, recording studio, arts centre, hot glass studio, training centre, a school, HeartFM community radio station, a nine-hole golf course, tennis court, swimming centre, playground, free electric barbecues and 24-hour public toilets.[70]

Occasionally, a monastery or church has surrounding land that can be farmed and developed to include guest accommodation, work placements, shops and art exhibitions.

VILLAGES OF GOD AS PIECEMEAL INTERCONNECTIONS IN AN AREA

With God, the piecemeal way is not as naive as it may at first appear. The American independent pastor Paul Sparks broadcasts his discoveries of how powerful the gospel can be when it takes root in the context of a place, at the intersection of geography, demography, economy and culture. He acknowledges that his is not a new idea—the concept of a parish is as old as Paul's letters to the various communities of the ancient church—but, in an age of dislocation and disengagement, the notion of a church that knows its place and gives itself to the place where it finds itself is like a breath of fresh air, like a sign of new life. He encourages people who drive to a church from elsewhere to take an interest in the neighbourhood that surrounds the church building and to ask what are the signs of God at work there. These signs may include the witness of Christians from other churches, but also people of goodwill who run shops, clubs, services and planning departments. Sparks writes:

When faith communities begin connecting together, in and for the neighbourhood, they learn to depend on God for strength to love, forgive and show grace like never before... The gospel becomes so much more tangible and compelling when the local church is actually a part of the community, connected to the struggles of the people, and even the land itself.[71]

Paul Sparks, Tim Soerens and Dwight J. Friesen have seen examples of this in cities, suburbs and small towns all over North America.

Christians can build into a secular shopping centre village by placing an eating, praying and listening space there. While I was residing in an Australian suburb for two weeks, I walked to the new shopping centre, which was advertised as a village. There I shopped, ate, read newspapers and relaxed in the park. Then I travelled to see the bishop of the local diocese. His office was hidden away from the public gaze. 'The bishop should have his headquarters in the village,' someone said. Two reasons could be cited against this: it would cost too much to rent or purchase offices, and the bishop is too busy to talk to locals. But suppose the diocese placed a prayer room and a volunteer 'pavement pastors' team in the shopping village, plus a thrift shop and café to pay for the rent? Some existing shopping centre villages include a traditional, underused church building, which could install prayer stations and provide a pilgrim trail.

A pioneer minister told me he was exploring the possibility of engaging with just two elements of a village of God, one at the hub and one on the fringe. The hub possibility was daily prayer by a core group in a church building that would otherwise become redundant. The fringe activity was a football club for Ghanaians. The faith element was that both hub and fringe activities might bear fruit and multiply, and might eventually connect up.

The value of this piecemeal approach is that any church member may do something, even if they are not a leader. They may build a good relationship with a hotdog vendor or a social service provider. The value of this model for church leaders is that it gives them a key that can open doors to fruitful ministry for the rest of their lives.

I have been astonished at the number of church leaders in isolated rural areas who are excited by the 'village of God' concept. It gives them hope and a methodology. They plot every Christian presence in a sparse region: a house group, a school, a ministry to old people, an after-school club, a farm with compassionate principles, a church, a chapel, a food bank, a B&B run by Christians. They develop relationships, share information leaflets and make a virtual village on a website. If they are in a tourist walking area, they make a pilgrim train.

VILLAGES OF GOD THAT GROW AROUND A HUB CHURCH

Most villages of God will grow from a hub church that creates transforming relationships with resource providers in the marketplace around them, as yeast transforms dough. Most towns and certain suburbs have at least one hub church, in the sense that the church building has spaces for functions such as prayer, events and eating. Examples are Birmingham's St Martin in the Bull Ring and London's St Martin-in-the-Fields at Trafalgar Square, which has daily crypt prayer, a café and shop, a centre for the homeless and spaces for concerts, lectures and exhibitions. The Oasis network typically has a Christian Academy School, a social project and a community church as a threefold hub in a needy urban community. Even a church building with limited uses, such as St

Michael le Belfrey in York, which has three Sunday congregations, has also spawned an arts church in a café, Alpha courses on student campuses and a youth facility in a hired venue.

However, I believe that a hub church is not meant to be a thing in itself, but a heart for the wider community around it. It is meant to be like the hub of a wheel, with spokes that touch every facet of life. In a multi-choice society, people want multiple connecting points that only a village of God can supply.

Hub churches that wish to spawn a village of God serve and build good relationships with the people in their locality, and members work in the world outside. They serve, not oust, the institutions that exist in their areas, inspiring in them values such as trust, spirituality and service. In this spirit, a traditional church building can publicise in its entrance porch what the church is for, how best to use its resources, and where to find local eating, accommodation and information places. As monasteries once set aside one or more people to oversee hospitality, so now representatives of a village of God invite neighbours to a celebration or open house. Café and shop staff, cyclists and allotment holders, charity workers and clubbers, taxi drivers and street gangs, fitness coaches and elderly people, office workers and bankers are all included. They invite musicians to busk, artists to exhibit their pictures, and youngsters to display their physical or poetic talents. Such developments can only take place where local people welcome them.

COMPONENTS OF A VILLAGE OF GOD

In my book *High Street Monasteries* I explored 'spaces' that a village of God might embrace. The hub of a village needs to include praying, meeting and eating spaces. Further out may be work, art, music, healing, guest, exercise and play spaces, plus facilities such as a Godly Play atrium, wifi study area and craft workshops. Green spaces might include community gardens, compostable products, wild areas and farms. Social and special needs, as well as upmarket housing, are natural components of a village of God, as are cooperatives and solar, wind, earth or water energy projects. Silent, meditation and learning spaces may be near to green spaces.[72]

As I travel, I meet people who want to add to this list. I shared in a house church that, after lunch, engaged in wrestling in the park opposite and urged me to add a wrestling arena to my 'village of God' chart! This is not as 'way out' as it might seem. The sixth-century Irish saint Abban, who is associated with a cell on the Isle of Jura, was sent by his father, a king, to be fostered and instructed in feats of strength and valour.[73] A twelve-month La Trobe University research project—the first in the world to measure the social impact of common sports—found that wrestling and other sports increased social connectedness, well-being, mental health, status, employment, persona and worth. The survey involved over 11,000 clubs and received 1677 responses. In holistic villages of God, not just in Buddhist centres, well-being of body and soul are linked.[74]

Other suggested additions to a village of God include prayer stations, clubs and credit unions, healthy food bakeries, twelve-step programmes for addiction recovery, prayer rooms for Muslims, car boot sales, parish nurses, cash machines, busking, prayer trees, massage, spa, cinema, interfaith and ethnic dialogue rooms, art exhibitions, libraries, interactive worship on big screens, and land care experiments. The revival of 'The Abbey' on Raymond Island in Australia's Gippsland Diocese has begun with a land-care project. Some villages of God might emulate Oslo, which is developing a 'bee highway'.

An example of a hub church that has spokes into the surrounding region is Northern Ireland's Causeway Coast Vineyard Church, Coleraine, which seeks to 'wash the feet of the city'. It offers healing in the streets, and groups that serve social needs along the coast, as well as groups for personal spiritual growth. It asked a local school, 'How can we serve you?' The school needed approved volunteers to assist with playground watch. The church earned the school's trust; now, suitable members also contribute to teaching and worship, and the church has transferred its Sunday school to the school site.[75]

In Preston Pans, Scotland, Scott Brennan, a church leader who follows the Community of Aidan and Hilda Way of Life, started some small culture-sensitive missional groups. Then the local Episcopal church, which became redundant, gave them first choice to buy the building. Scott's groups are treating it as a hub for an embryo village of God. The village provides youth activities, including a School of Rock, and a worship area, with hopes to establish daily prayer in an upper room, a café and a healing room. A community garden is being developed and the building has become the venue for the Three Harbours Arts Festival. Scott visited his local councillor. 'Help me to listen to the needs of the area,' he said. 'There is a gap in provision for people with mental health issues,' the councillor told him, so now a mental health support programme is in place. The councillor is a great supporter of the church, which hosts a regular meeting with local public service agencies.

When a lone, struggling church in another area asks Scott what they can do, he suggests that they look for partners. Scott works with missional leaders throughout Scotland, including The Cairn, with its vision for such developments throughout the Celtic lands. He says of villages of God based on Aidan and Hilda's style of values and rhythms, 'Ten years ago the ideal was charismatic churches in warehouses; today the ground is ready for this vision to take root.'[76]

VALUES OF A VILLAGE OF GOD

The glue of a village of God is not attendance; it is a way of life, which people can relate to at different levels. A core group will make life commitments to it, while those on the fringe respect the ethos. If the village of God, whether it is in a geographical or a virtual space, has seven-days-a-week transformative prayer at its heart, it is possible to have things going on in the outskirts that meet a 'non-spiritual' need. People feel at home. It is a safe space for them, where trust can grow.

Because a village of God seeks the common good and values relationships of trust with all people of goodwill, sooner or later, as it is able, it connects with agencies such as social services, hospitals, schools, shops, eating places, police, nightclubs, gangs, charities, local government, business and leisure centres, as well as Christian groups and ministries.

What is the point of connections with such institutions? In the UK, as in other countries, government inspectors require staff in public services to hit frequently changing productivity targets, which can cause exhaustion and disillusionment among staff. One staff member said to me, 'The one thing they never check up on is whether the children are loved.' The same applies to hospital patients. The more such public services are nourished within a context of prayer and love, the better they become. As ever more jobs are franchised out, citizens who suffer from breakdowns in provision feel powerless. There is no chain of command; each unit in the chain puts responsibility upon someone else. A village of God, as distinct from a single and marginalised church, has more influence with decision-makers. It may be able to secure good practice and speak up on behalf of the little person whose voice is not taken seriously.

Those who envision a village of God need to weave a fabric of trust. Aidan's ability to establish a cohesive, transformative community that did not rule out apostolic callings merits high regard. Aidan worked with people of contrasting traditions— Queen Elfreda and Wilfred at Lindisfarne, Hilda at Hartlepool and Oswin at York. He worked with Picts, Britons and English. He empowered others, such as the four brothers Caelin, Cedd,

Chad and Cynebil. If churches aspire to be places of heart, home and hub within the postmodern context, who knows what may emerge when people with this vision offer leadership in the spirit of Aidan?

Unlike a typical Irish monastic settlement, which was incidentally missional in the sense that people came and went and were transformed, Aidan's English monastic settlements were intentionally missional. As far as we can tell, they sent out faith-sharing brothers into the highways and byways. Bede records as much of Lindisfarne and Whitby, and Cuthbert's missionary journeys, undertaken while he was still a monk at Melrose, suggest that this was the tradition there.

These examples contrast with Benedictine and later monastic enclosures that kept monks separate from the unchurched people outside. A village of God with an Aidan ethos can subsume and transform the four models of mission with which this chapter began. For most of Christian history, pastoral care came from monasteries. In a village with varied facets, there is something to attract most people. It is true that many people in our unredeemed society want to partake of something rather than belong to it. Pilgrimage enables this, and villages of God can link up with each other and with sacred sites to nudge pilgrims into a larger sense of belonging.

A village of God may seem small, but history has been changed by transformative cells. The Bible portrays the significance of a remnant who, by doing God's will, turn a corner of history. Arnold Toynbee, in his *History of Civilisation*, calls them a 'creative minority'. There is a tremendous power in being a minority guided by God.

REFLECTION

I imagine Aidan arriving on Lindisfarne with Oswald's helpers and his twelve brothers. Before they arrive, he has soaked it in prayer—its contours, viewpoints, sheltered and crossing places, its soils and rocks. He has envisaged how the parts can best be located to work together for the whole. He has a mind for the future, for growth. He sees it as a cradle—a cradle of faith and farming, of learning and community, of hospitality and art. He prays for the whole of Northumbria. He sees such cradle places springing into being in the mouths of rivers and at inland crossing places. The Anglo-Saxons knew only forts and conquests. Aidan knew deep down that these villages of God were meant to replace the forts in the affections of the people, until the people's hearts were conquered by love.

'Think global, act local.' What kind of world do you see as you pray, 'Your kingdom come on earth as it is in heaven'? How can this macrocosm be reflected in the microcosm of your locality? What elements of a village of God can you identify in your church, neighbouring churches, projects and agencies of goodwill? How might they be inspired by the vision, embrace the values, establish working relationships and take a next step?

This prayer for such places can be sung to the tune 'Danny Boy':

Here be the peace of those who do your sacred will;
here be the praise of God by night and day;
here be the place where strong ones serve the weakest,
here be a sight of Christ's most gentle way.

Here be the strength of prophets righting greed and wrong,
here be the green of land that's tilled with love;
here be the soil of holy lives maturing,
here be a people one with all the saints above.

WOMEN AND THE SPIRITUAL FOSTER MOTHERS

THE TWELVE WERE WITH HIM, AS WELL AS SOME
WOMEN WHO HAD BEEN CURED... AND MANY OTHERS
WHO PROVIDED FOR THEM OUT OF THEIR RESOURCES.
(LUKE 8:1-3)

Bede, our main source for Aidan among the English, did not
honour women, and they play only a marginal role in his *Ecclesiastical History*, so we have to put together pieces in a jigsaw and
make deductions. The two big pieces of evidence are that spiritual
foster mothers played a pivotal role in the spiritual formation
of Aidan's Ireland[77] and came to play a pivotal role in Aidan's
spiritual formation of the English.[78]

At Ireland's great Rock of Cashel is a carving of St Brigid
presiding over the twelve apostles. Apocryphal stories tell of
her being consecrated a bishop by a short-sighted bishop who,
overwhelmed by the sheet of fire above her head, read the wrong
form of words! A somewhat more historical story is that Brigid
put Bishop Conleath in charge of the men's quarters in her
double monastery of men and women at Kildare: she ruled over
all. Brigid founded many small women's monasteries. Stories of
Brigid would have circulated in Aidan's Ireland, as did stories of

the spiritual foster mothers. Fosterage of the children of chiefs and landowners was part of Ireland's culture. Under Christianity, these spiritual foster parents embraced multitudes. They were the glory of Ireland.

In the sixth century, Ita became known as 'the foster mother of the saints of Ireland'. Many children were sent to her school and community at Killeady, south of Limerick. Ita said she wanted to hold in her hands and foster, not the children of chiefs and clerics but Jesus, the Son of God himself, in all the children she fostered. Ita's closeness to Jesus and Mary was the secret of her work. A hymn has come down to us, attributed to Ita:

> *It is Jesus who is nursed by me in my little hermitage.*
> *It is Jesus, with those who dwell in heaven,*
> *whom I hold against my heart each night.*[79]

Aidan would most probably have known stories of Brendan, the son of a Christian couple of royal blood near Tralee. The aged Bishop Erc placed him in the care of Ita. When Brendan asked her what three works were most pleasing and what were most displeasing to God, Ita replied, 'The three things that please God are true faith in God with a pure heart, a simple life with a grateful spirit, and a generosity inspired by love. The three things that most displease God are a mouth that hates people, a heart harbouring resentments, and putting reliance upon wealth.' Ita affirmed Brendan in his desire to leave home and embark on an adventure, telling him, 'A foreign land is calling you so that you can instruct the souls of those over there.'[80] It seems, however, that Brendan did not consult his soul friend over practical matters, for when he returned from his first voyage, somewhat disillusioned with the setbacks they had suffered, Ita rebuked him for not consulting her about how to make the boats.

We have no way of knowing whether Aidan knew the Irish legend, put into writing by Christian monks, of Emer, who became the wife of hero Cu Chulainn. She vowed she would only marry the man who was her equal in noble birth, beauty and wisdom. She was said to have the six gifts of womanhood: beauty, chastity, needlework, sweet speech, voice and wisdom. Her story is retold in W.B. Yeats' play *The Only Jealousy of Emer*.

We learn from Bede's *Life of Cuthbert* that Cuthbert had a spiritual mother named Kenswith. He went to visit her during his missionary travels as a monk at Melrose. There is some evidence that wealthy pagan Anglo-Saxons sent their children to be educated by foster parents, but they would not have been spiritual foster parents in the Christian sense. Kenswith suggests that the Christian spiritual mother had crept into the English way of life.

Aidan began to receive women into vows. He asked Hieu, who came from Ireland and took vows as a nun, to establish a small monastic group of women at Hartlepool. He may have received the vows of Bega, who, according to her medieval *Life*, fled a rapist in Ireland and established a community of nuns at what is now St Bees, Cumbria.

ST HILDA

The big breakthrough came through Aidan's friendship with the English princess, Hild (Hilda in modern English). She had become a baptised Christian through the Roman missionary Paulinus, under the rule of her great-uncle, King Edwin. When Edwin was slain, Paulinus fled to Kent and most of his converts returned to their pagan gods, but Hilda remained true. Hilda was deeply impressed by Aidan, his teaching, and the way of life of the Irish mission. She lived their spirituality for the rest of her life.

Hilda's sister Hereswith married into the East Anglian royal family, who were devout Christians. Hilda, desiring a more contemplative and intentional Christian life, stayed with them for at least a year. In due course, her sister joined the monastery of Chelles, in what is now France. A unique development had taken place among the Franks. In the wake of the Irish monk Columbanus' foundations for men, which were popular for their ascetic but human ways, the aristocratic women wanted this style of community for themselves, too. Some of them became abbesses of double monasteries for women and men.

Aidan heard that Hilda intended to follow her sister and take vows as a nun at Chelles. We may surmise that something jumped inside him. Hilda wished to go there because he could offer her nothing similar among the English, yet he longed that he could. God put an idea into his head. It was a high risk and quite beyond normal church protocol. He sent a message to Hilda. Its gist was this: 'Please change your plans. Return to Northumbria and help us pioneer such monasteries for women and men here.'

Hilda agreed to return. Instead of a formal noviciate among the Franks, she received informal support among the Irish and English. Aidan and other learned brothers visited her frequently, instructed her assiduously and loved her heartily for her innate wisdom and her devotion to God's service. Once again, relationship triumphed over regulation.

Aidan gave her a plot of land on the north side of the River Wear, possibly on the site of today's Monkwearmouth. It was a laboratory for her and a few companions. It outgrew itself within a year. Aidan's friend Heiu desired to leave the little community at Hart's Pool (Hartlepool) on the coastal headland over 100 miles south of Lindisfarne and live as a solitary, probably at what is now Tadcaster. Aidan asked Hilda to take charge of this community, and she developed it into a double community of men and women. After Aidan's death, Hilda was asked to build up a larger double community of women and men further south along the east coast, at Whitby. In both places she poured her energy into establishing a pattern that shone with values such as justice, devotion, purity, peace and love. Her students were required to spend regular times in the study of the scriptures, and also in good works among the people (*EH* 4.23).

In her book *Anglo-Saxon Women and the Church*, Stephanie Hollis acknowledges the sparsity and prejudice of Bede's references to women. She combs through references in the *Anglo-Saxon Chronicle*, Aldhelm, and the *Lives* of Wilfred, Cuthbert and Leoba in order to garner insights. Aldhelm furnishes us with information about the nuns at Barking, among the East Saxons whom Cedd of Lindisfarne evangelised. Aldhem likens the nuns to soldiers of Christ. He urges recruits to fight with muscular energy against pride and the seven virulent vices. They are to exercise their minds through assiduous reading; they are to be wrestlers in a gymnasium and panting runners seeking to win a race. In a warrior society, these practices no doubt attracted more recruits. They read about the desert fathers in Cassian's writings. For them, community was vital: Aldhelm likens the nuns to a swarm of bees.

Hollis writes of a kinship with the Holy Spirit in Hilda's monastery: 'Virtue spread by oral report, action at a distance, the mysterious influence of goodness without discernible human agency.'[81] These monasteries became little towns where all human activities took place in an atmosphere of prayer.

I was invited to speak about 'Saint Hilda, reconciliation and the future of the church' at a colloquium at the Anglican Centre in Rome. Representatives of New Zealand/Aoroteara's Anglican church spoke about the approach of its Maori wing. It was more intuitive, less bookbound and more relational, and the Maoris had no word for 'enemy'. Lecturers from Rome's Gregorian University spoke about their evangelisation work in various African countries. 'Anthropology is as important as ecclesiology,' they said; 'dreams and intuition play an important role.' I spoke about a Celtic dimension of the church as lived by St Hilda, who was esteemed as a 'merciful mother' by both Irish and Roman advocates. Disagreement within the church is not a reason for splitting or excluding. The test of how Christian we are is how we relate to Christ in our brother and sister Christians (1 John 4:21).

For a thousand years after the demise of Hilda's and similar double monasteries of women and men led by an abbess in France and Germany, no commensurate roles were open to women. With Christendom facing a turning point in our own day, the colloquium in Rome discussed the question 'What now?' One view was that Jesus our high priest was the Son of Man—that is, the representative of all humanity—so a priesthood that represents only half the human race is less than fully catholic. Another view was that mothers, unlike fathers, need to provide wholehearted nurture of their baby during its life in the womb, at the breast, and for some time afterwards. The high calling of motherhood needs protection from careerism. This leaves unanswered the question: what about unmarried spiritual mothers?

I asked about the role of women in Rome. 'No one listens to women in the Vatican,' said someone who works there. 'John Paul II agreed to a change in the constitution of the Focolare movement, which includes male priests. This stipulated that a woman shall always lead it,' said another. John Paul II was devoted to the theologian von Balthazar, who had a woman as his muse, said someone else; and another thought that he himself consulted a female muse. A pilgrim told me that a prophetess whom John Paul II often consulted gave him a copy of my book *Exploring Celtic Spirituality*. So I asked, 'Does anyone know of a woman muse or of a figure like Hilda in Rome?' No one knew.

We need a theology that honours the divine image in all—women and men alike.

Oswin, the tall, handsome and popular king of the restored subkingdom of Deira, invited Aidan to spend more time with him at his headquarters in York. According to Symeon of Durham, what he termed the archbishopric of York was placed under Aidan and his successors for 30 years.

Although Oswin knew that Aidan walked whenever he could, he gave him an expensive royal horse for emergencies and for crossing rivers. Shortly afterwards, Aidan and his team met a beggar who asked for some money with which to buy food. Aidan, a compassionate 'father of the poor', gave the horse and all its expensive trappings to the beggar. Before the meal back at the king's place, someone told Oswin what Aidan had done. Oswin was furious. 'You had no right to give to that beggar a priceless gift I chose specifically for you as bishop,' he fumed. 'I have plenty of other gifts you can distribute to the poor.' 'Surely,' Aidan replied, 'that son of a mare is not more precious to you than that son of God?'

Oswin warmed himself by the fire and pondered Aidan's words. Suddenly he gave his sword to a thane, flung himself at Aidan's feet and said, 'Forgive me. Never again will I question what you do with anything I give you; nor will I question how much you give to children of God' (*EH* 3.14).

In this story is hidden the essence of humanism. It echoes the teaching of John 1:4: Christ is the light within every human being. It reflects Genesis 1:27: the likeness of male and female together is God's image in humanity. By our creation, every woman and every man is made in God's image and is therefore of infinite worth. Sin mars that image and sabotages a God-filled life. That is why we all need Jesus to sift out the sin, to purify us until only the gold—that which is of God in us—is left. We will not mirror God to the world until men and women work in a partnership that frees each to come to his or her full flower.

Aidan's mission lifted women from being the playthings and servants of a brutal warrior. Iona also played a part in improving women's conditions. Its Abbot Adomnan (d.704) had a vision of an angel who said to him, 'Make a law in Ireland and Britain that a woman cannot be killed in any manner.' What is now known as Adomnan's Law makes it illegal to force a woman or a child to fight in a battle.

Yet in the history of Christianity so far, only three countries have routinely dignified women by appointing them to lead large monasteries of men and women: France, England and Germany. These monasteries died out after Viking invasion and Norman colonisation. For more than 1000 years after Hilda, women were again belittled. The more recent struggle for the dignity of women has been strong and unequal; in some Muslim countries it has barely begun. In Western lands where women's liberation has passed into law, these gains have sometimes been marred by women who hate men or reject their own femininity. Hardness demeans womanhood and is no substitute for the strength of suppleness and the beauty of insight.

Aidan's mission liberated women from a life of misery as the property of men who fought battles in summer and bragged about their exploits as they boozed in winter. He opened up a route that enabled them to live their dreams, to find sanctuary and education. The women monastics then empowered other women and men to live their dreams.

REFLECTION

I imagine Aidan thinking back to his own spiritual foster mother (whom we may assume he most probably had) during his childhood in Ireland and recalling lessons he had learned. I imagine him retelling stories of these great spiritual foster mothers during his frequent visits as mentor to Hilda. He knew, as we may know, that spiritual mothers can be wellsprings of wisdom, reaching parts of human beings that others cannot reach. Within the rhythms of prayer and nature, they connected the personal quest to live in the heart of Christ with the quest for the church to become Christ's heart for its neighbourhood.

In recent years, the concept of 'spiritual intelligence' has come to the fore. This is the apex of a pyramid built on simpler forms of intelligence: IQ, emotional intelligence and social intelligence. Spiritual intelligence includes awareness of the frames of reference of oneself and others, a centre of compassion and empathy that transfigures them, and an ability to maintain calm and equilibrium in all circumstances. These are the qualities associated with the Messiah (Isaiah 11:2), which he wishes to impart to his people. I hope that we can develop wellsprings of wisdom and spiritual nurturing that disciple people in these qualities. Think through how to begin such an endeavour.

People of clashing views looked to Hilda as a 'merciful mother'. Cindy Wigglesworth's book *SQ21* explores 21 components of spiritual intelligence. How can we cultivate it in our own lives?

Think about each street in your locality. Does it have a potential mother figure—someone who keeps her ear to the ground and embraces or encourages people of every background, someone to whom people go with their troubles? How can natural nurturers be introduced to Christian wellsprings of wisdom?

Star-kindler, Pain-bearer,
Give us grace to accept the gifts you delight to shower upon us:
Gifts of wisdom and nurture,
Gifts of friendship and understanding,
Gifts of reflection and creativity,
Gifts of earthiness and trust,
Until you restore the garment of our self-respect
and remake us in your beauty.

RULE AND RHYTHM

WE ARE WHAT WE REPEATEDLY DO. EXCELLENCE,
THEN, IS NOT AN ACT, BUT A HABIT.

ARISTOTLE[82]

I ascended Kuala Lumpur's tourist Viewing Tower, entered its prayer room and read a booklet for visitors. A Muslim authority described the meaning of religion. For Christians, he explained, it meant going to a church service on Sundays; for Muslims it meant a way of life. That is the tragedy of Christianity. Could Islam be a John the Baptist movement to recall Christians to a way of life?

Christianity began as a way of life. The first Christians followed the daily hours of prayer and were called followers of the Way (Acts 9:2; 18:25; 22:4; 24:14), but soon, for many, this religion became clericalised and ritualised—a Sunday thing. Bede, however, informs us of something hugely significant. Six centuries after Christ, Aidan introduced a Rule to the English people: 'Churches were built in diverse places; the people joyfully flocked together to hear the Word; lands and other property were given of the king's bounty to found monasteries; English children, as well as their elders, were instructed by their (Irish) teachers in study and the observance of the discipline of a Rule' (*EH* 3.3). Aidan's disciple Cedd became bishop of the East Saxons and gathered people in two places: 'The first of these places is on the bank of the Pant, the other on the bank of the Thames.

In these, gathering a flock of Christ's servants, he taught them to observe the discipline of a rule of life, as far as those rude people were then capable of receiving it' (*EH* 3.22).

A RULE OR A WAY?

Once again, as in the New Testament, onlookers could observe that Christians were followers of the Way. Bede, writing through a Roman lens two generations after Aidan, uses the Latin word *regula*, from which comes words such as 'rule', 'ruler', 'regular' and 'regulation', to describe what Aidan's mission introduced. By his time, Benedict Biscop had created a written Rule at Monkwearmouth, which was an amalgam of various monastic regulations he had encountered on the Continent as well as in Northumbria. Yet the examples that Bede gives from Aidan's mission suggest patterns and practices rooted more in relationship than regulation, including the practice of daily prayer, alms giving and good deeds to one's neighbour (*EH* 3.5). Those inside monasteries had further disciplines, such as fasting, but the monasteries were of the people and for the people. So whether this people's 'Rule of life' came through the monasteries or through Christians like Aidan, who walked among the people, it was in some measure organic and indivisible.

Were these 'Rules', at least in the monasteries, written down? If so, they have not survived. The earliest recorded Rules of monasteries in Celtic lands are from the eighth century.[83] The founder or their successor was the Rule: he or she led by example and verbal guidance. Yet we know that the Iona library had writings of Basil of Caesarea in its library. Basil (d.379) wrote a Rule for monks. He believed that a monk was, in principle, what every Christian was meant to be. His monks invited orphans into their communities. Penitentials have survived—ascetic training programmes for monks, which helped them overcome vices and grow in virtues. It seems likely that this approach was also used in a more flexible way with Christians who had not made vows.[84]

Columbanus, a contemporary of Iona's Columba, did write Rules that have survived, for pioneer missionary monks, though these Rules were stricter than those for people in settled conditions. A study of Columbanus' writings reveals that he was steeped in both of Cassian's books about the fourth-century desert fathers. Cassian's books were known at Iona. He wrote his *Institutes* for those who would war against the destructive inner demons, and his *Conferences* to excite others to a life of contemplation and compassion. Something of these desert monastic disciplines was surely brought to the English by Aidan.

So the Rule that Aidan brought to the English was rooted in Basil and Cassian, lightened by the loving nature of the Irish extended families, and adapted to the practicalities and nature of the English. Benedict's more formalised Rule had not yet reached the English.

Aidan mentored Hilda. Bede tells us that when she was put in charge of the monastic community for women and men at Hartlepool:

[Hilda] began immediately to order it in all things under a rule of life; and taught there the strict observance of justice, piety, chastity, and other virtues, and particularly of peace and charity; so that, after the example of the primitive Church, no one there was rich, and none poor, for they had all things in common. None had any private property... She obliged those who were under her direction to give so much time to reading of the Holy Scriptures, and to exercise themselves so much in works of justice. (EH 3.23)

Bede writes that Eata, who, as a boy, trained at Aidan's Lindisfarne school, sent Cuthbert to be prior of Lindisfarne because of the example of Cuthbert's own practice, and to instruct the brothers in the observance of regular discipline (*EH* 3.27). When Cuthbert was dying on Inner Farne Isle, he admonished the brothers to preserve the virtues of love and peace among themselves and towards all the faithful, and with unwearied earnestness to follow the rules of monastic discipline, which they had either been taught by him and had seen him observe or had found in the words and actions of the former fathers (*EH* 2.3).

Chad, another of Aidan's first students, 'endeavoured to instruct his people by the same manner of life and character, after his and his own brother Cedd's example'. He took no other sustenance than a small piece of bread, one hen's egg and a little milk and water. This, he said, was the custom of those of whom he had learned the rule of regular discipline (*EH* 3.28). Elsewhere, Bede tells us that 'many religious men and women, led by Aidan's example, adopted the custom of prolonging their fast on Wednesdays and Fridays until the evening, throughout the year, except during the fifty days after Easter'.

As we piece together such references, we get a picture of a popular movement, engined by the people's monasteries, that patterned prayer and fasting, justice and learning as a way of life (*EH* 1.23).

THE RHYTHM OF IN AND OUT

If your output exceeds your input, then your upkeep will be your downfall. (Anon)

The pattern of outreach and withdrawal, advance and retreat, was another key feature of Aidan's, as of Christ's, way of life. It sometimes brought about a spiritual authority that could affect looming disaster in the outside world.

Aidan made a habit of retiring to the Inner Farne Isle, from which he could see the royal garrison at Bamburgh, to pray in solitude and silence. A notable miracle took place during one of these retreats, showing that, far from being a withdrawal from engagement, regular retreats can spawn prayer that can change the course of events.

The hostile army of the Mercians, under the command of Penda, cruelly ravaged the Northumbrians and reached the royal city. Being unable to take it by storm or by siege, Penda endeavoured to burn it down. Having pulled down all the neighbouring buildings, he brought an immense quantity of beams, rafters, partitions, wattles and thatch, piled them to a great height on the land side and, when the wind was favourable, set light to the pile in order to burn down the garrison. When Aidan saw the flames and smoke rising above the walls, he lifted up his eyes and hands to heaven and cried with tears, 'Look, Lord, how great an evil is wrought by Penda!' These words were hardly uttered when the wind, immediately veering from the garrison, drove back the flames upon those who had kindled them, so that some being hurt and all afraid, they fled, believing that place to be protected by the hand of God.

We, like Aidan, need a pattern of retreat in order to advance. The danger of mission today is that we need success. Thomas Merton wrote, 'The job of being a success in today's competitive world leaves no time for compassion.'[85] Prayer becomes a back-up, not the engine of God's work. Even John Maxwell, whose books on principles of leadership have become world bestsellers, recognises in his *The Fifteen Invaluable Laws of Growth* that 'learning to pause allows growth to catch up with you'.[86]

ASCETIC PRACTICES AND THE HERMITS OF INNIS CATHAIG

It is possible that Aidan learned the ways of monastic withdrawal followed by outreach early in life in Ireland. The 17th-century *Martyrology of Donegal* lists Aidan's first bishopric as Inis Cathaig—Scattery Island, where hermits had lived for generations. Canon John O'Hanlon, in Volume 8 of his monumental series *The Lives of the Irish Saints*, assumes that Aidan of Scattery and Aidan of Lindisfarne are the same person.[87] Versions of the *Catholic*

Encyclopedia and the *Encyclopedia Britannica* have given credence to this tradition.

At the least, the identification of Aidan of Lindisfarne with Aidan of Inis Cathaig indicates that our Aidan's life and work were well-known and admired in his native Ireland. The Martyrologies of Tallagh and Cashel, the Annals of Roscrea, and nearly all medieval documents attest to it. The statement of the Scholist on the *Feilire of St Aengus* has Aidan as the son of Lugar, son to Ernin, son of Cael, son to Aed, son of Artchorp, son of Niacorp. The O'Clerys state that he sprang from the tribe of Eochaidh Finn Fuath nairt, from whom St Brigid descends.[88]

The dates in these records would have been guesses, with a margin of error of a generation, but the stated chronology is not impossible, and I know locals near Scattery who firmly accept this tradition. However, Scattery was not part of the Columba family of monasteries, though links of friendship may have developed. We know that Columba established a line of midland monasteries which lay on a major route from Munster into the north of Ireland—Tihilly, Lynally, Drumcullen, Kinnitty, Seir Kieran, Birr and Roscrea. It seems unlikely that a monk from one of these monasteries would be given oversight of Scattery— unless perhaps the Scattery monks had problems and asked them for help, in which case Aidan's legendary discretion might explain such a posting.

Scattery was founded by Senan, of whom more than one *Life* survives. Senan had sought out teachers in Britain and Gaul and had become a learned teacher. Some regarded him as one of the Twelve Apostles of Ireland. He founded communities in the mouths of rivers. His sister had a vision of pillars of fire towering above the monastic communities of Ireland, and the highest pillar of all was that above Senan's island at Scattery. Senan was noted for his devotion to fasting, even as a child, and for his ascetic lifestyle.

If Aidan spent years on an island where the ascetic ideals of the desert Christians were the main focus, spiritual practices that led to inner transformation would have been taken deep into his being. Even if he did not, the impulse to hermit life was strong among the Irish during the period of Aidan and within Columba's monasteries.

If Aidan was at Scattery, we may have to revise the assumption that he was a junior to Corman, the leader of the first failed mission to Lindisfarne. An alternative portrayal emerges of him as a senior heavyweight, whom Iona was willing to lose only when it became clear that less experienced monks, such as Corman, were not up to the challenge. Whichever was the case, there is little doubt that meditation was central to the way of life of Aidan and his disciples. Bede refers to Egbert, who as a youth trained with Chad in Ireland, and 'long and zealously led a monastic life... in prayer and self-denial and meditation on the Holy Scriptures' (*EH* 4.5).

Part of Aidan's Rule was the wearing of the monk's tonsure. Although Aidan and his monks were culture-friendly, they did not eschew all symbols of the monastic life. Aidan wore simple woollen clothes. His monks cut off their front hair in common with the universal monastic tradition, but, unlike Roman monks, they could allow their hair to grow long at the back. Celts loved long, flowing hair. A similar issue has arisen within my own Community of Aidan and Hilda. Each person who takes vows is asked to thoughtfully wear, carry or display the Community Cross. Some think this puts off people in a particular locality, so they do not wear it. It is important to be clear that Aidan's monks did not pretend to be who they were not. Not being oneself may cause more confusion and ultimate disappointment. The people grew to love Aidan's monks because they loved others while remaining true to their monastic calling.

Aidan's way of life was, above all else, a relationship of healing love with God, people and the earth, into which everyone was invited.

Today's world requires a sensitive, humble monasticism that is of the people, by the people and for the people. What might a 'People's Rule of Life' in the spirit of Aidan look like today?

In recent decades, new grassroots monastic movements have emerged, one of which has named itself The Community of Aidan and Hilda.[89] It invites people to earth their following of Christ in a Way of Life that is a journey with a soul friend. This springs from an abandonment to the unconditional communion of love at the heart of the triune God. So they first of all commit to three 'life-giving principles', which help them strip away anything that usurps that love: simplicity ('Blessed are the poor in spirit', Matthew 5:3), purity of motive ('Blessed are the pure in heart', v. 8) and obedience to God in the other person ('Blessed are the meek', v. 5).

These principles stand out in Aidan's mission.

- Simplicity: The prelate Wilfred, while dismissing at the Synod of Whitby the Irish beliefs about such things as the date of Easter, nevertheless confessed, 'I do not deny those also to have been God's servants, and beloved of God, who with rude simplicity, but pious intentions, have themselves loved Him' (*EH* 3.24).

- Purity, or authenticity: '(Aidan) taught nothing that he did not practise in his life among his brethren; for he neither sought nor loved anything of this world' (*EH* 3.5).

- Obedience: In the Irish tradition, contrary to ignorant assertions, a monk could not wander off at whim. While the task of spreading the gospel involved considerable periods away from home, such journeys could be made only with the permission of the abbot. Adomnan more than once tells us of Cormac Ua Liathain, abbot of Durrow, who sailed in search of a desert island. One of these voyages failed because he had in his company a monk who had left his monastery without his abbot's permission.[90] There is no hint that Aidan's monasteries dispensed with this kind of obedience, which has nothing to do with subservience but takes seriously the apostle Paul's advice: 'Let each of you look not to your own interests, but to the interests of others' (Philippians 2:4).

The Community of Aidan and Hilda invites followers to seek simplicity in what they speak and text (their 'yes' is 'yes' and their 'no' is 'no'), and in what they do (they do what God puts in their heart, not what their false ego and our crazed society call for). They seek simplicity in order to free their lives of whatever distracts them from mindfulness. They discard what clutters their spirits in order that they may be available to God and to share goods, money or time with needy people. They seek purity of motive in work, study and relationships so that affections are transparent and not divided. They seek to heed that which is of God in those who exercise any role, and therefore to honour God's authority.

The journey is aided by ten Waymarks such as lifelong learning, regular retreat, a rhythm of prayer, work and recreation, openness to others in listening, and sharing Jesus and justice.

Aidan, like monastics everywhere, taught the value of praying at various hours in the day, marked by the sun. Because the Irish approach did not distance inhouse practices from the awareness of God in creation, 'rhythm' perhaps best describes these practices. They are not extra luggage, nor are they legalistic; they represent a mindfulness that enables us to relax into the rhythms that God has put within creation and within us. They restore the naturalness of Adam and Eve walking with God in the garden of Eden.

David Cole, the Community of Aidan and Hilda's Guide for Explorers, suggests the following wider pattern in his book *The Mystic Path of Meditation: Beginning a Christ-centred journey*:

- Meditate momentarily: take times throughout the day to do this.
- Divert daily: focus attention on the Bible or other meditation.

- Withdraw weekly for an hour or two of silence.
- Make a date monthly for a day devoted to God alone.
- Abdicate annually: go to a monastery, retreat house or 'desert'.[91]

Followers of this and similar ways of life say to us something like this:

- As the sun rises, we rise with God and scripture.
- As the sun settles, we offload inner garbage, reflect and learn from the day, and settle down with God (the 'Examen').
- We create a weekly balance between work and prayer, exercise and social duties, recreation and study.
- We attune ourselves to the natural seasons, taking in more in winter, giving out more in summer, sharing each season with our soul friend.
- We attune ourselves to the Christian seasons, making a yearly retreat alone with God.

Members of some communities sign up to receive an automatic email or phone message to remind them of what they are all praying for at that time.[92]

What about Aidan's emphasis on fasting? Christians today apply the principle of fasting in more varied ways. Some fast from the internet or car-driving at specific times. Certain Christians fast during Ramadan in order to be in solidarity with their Muslim neighbours. A parish priest tells me he has 'cracked' workaholism by fasting until 3.00 pm on weekdays during the three Celtic 40-day 'Lents' before Christmas, before Easter and after Pentecost.

For postmodern people, everything is equally valid: 'You follow your religion and I follow my own path.' They are not challenged to wrestle with what is. Aidan did not take the path of relativism but of relationship. Aidan was sent by a branch of the one universal Church; he did not start something that was out of relationship with the rest of the body of Christ.

The political philosopher Alasdair MacIntyre famously closed his 1987 book, *After Virtue*, with a warning and a call:

A crucial turning point in that earlier history occurred when men and women of good will turned aside from the task of shoring up the Roman imperium and ceased to identify the continuation of civility and moral community with the maintenance of that imperium. What they set themselves to achieve instead— often not recognising fully what they were doing—was the construction of new forms of community within which the moral life could be sustained so that both morality and civility might survive the coming ages of barbarism and darkness. If my account of our moral condition is correct [one characterised by moral incoherence and unsettlable moral disputes in the modern world], we ought to conclude that for some time now we too have reached that turning point. What matters at this stage is the construction of local forms of community within which civility and the intellectual and moral life can be sustained through the new dark ages which are already upon us. And if the tradition of the virtues was able to survive the horrors of the last dark ages, we are not entirely without grounds for hope. This time, however, the barbarians are not waiting beyond the frontiers; they have already been governing us for quite some time. And it is our lack of consciousness of this that constitutes part of our predicament. We are waiting not for a Godot, but for another—doubtless very different—St Benedict.[93]

I think MacIntyre is right that we need a monastic prototype, but one that is very different from Benedict. Benedict discouraged monks from travelling. If they gained permission to leave their enclosure, they were required not to speak of what they encountered outside because it might have a disruptive effect. Celtic monks, in contrast, if their requests were persistent and serious, were permitted to travel.

In England, there is another reason not to rush in to insensitive reconstructions of Benedictine communities. Many places still fester with 500 years of wounded memory, which can often be traced back to a Benedictine abbey or priory inhabited by foreigners who lorded it over the local peasant population. I know localities with Benedictine ruins where inhabitants are still resentful of 'foreigners' or incomers who bring their own alien agendas and are not at one with the local people.

I am told that bishops seek to bring back Benedictine expressions into the Church of England. When people feel that 'things fall apart, the centre cannot hold' (W.B. Yeats), it is understandable that they want to create some protected 'zones of stability'. But if God is in the falling apart, might he not want leaders to abandon themselves to the process and use tools that help them to navigate the ocean of flux without hitting the reefs? The Irish 'pilgrims for the love of God' who travelled across the continent did more to re-evangelise Dark Age Europe than the top-down missions or stay-put monasteries. Aidan and the Irish monks model a way of living amid 'the changes and chances' of this fleeting life. Their communities were not endpoints but launchpads. A Celtic Rule can combine the depths of ancient monastic disciplines with the flexibility of today's world.

REFLECTION

I imagine Aidan reviewing in his mind the patterns and disciplines of Irish monasteries he knew, and the Penitentials of Finnian and Columbanus. I imagine him recalling maxims of Columba, practices at Iona and guidelines introduced by his abbot Seghine. The English had none of these in their background, but the twelve who came with him from Ireland had. He would share the practices first with these brothers and then with the English, when they became school students or monastic brothers. Jesus shared with his twelve apostles. Aidan would share his own temptations and the way he had overcome them, the pitfalls and challenges he foresaw, and ways of sustaining the inner life when all else seemed to crumble. 'Take my yoke,' said Jesus; 'do as I do.' Daily prayer and scripture, regular outreach, fasting and retreats are all part of his example.

As Aidan pointed out at Iona's post-mortem on Corman's failed mission to the Northumbrians, they could not lay all these rules upon the untutored peasants outside the monasteries, who as yet knew only half the Gospels. Yet Aidan knew that grace is not hidden only in holy enclosures but also in the mundane routines of ordinary people's lives. If they did not take some holy habits into their souls, their homes and their local communities, their new faith would be but a house built on sand. Jesus gave the Beatitudes to the people as a whole. Simplicity, purity, obedience in giving alms and heeding God in the other person, a daily rhythm of prayer, Gospel reflection, work and service—these practices, the people could make their own.

What are the core values against which you evaluate your actions and attitudes? What prayer or meditation practices help to earth you in 'rhythms of grace'? Which corporate values and spiritual disciplines might you introduce to your faith community? What practices might be commended to the people in your neighbourhood?

Day by day, dear Lord, may we follow Jesus
By scripture's guidance
In soul friend's confidence
In the spirit of saints
In godly rhythms
In overcoming prayer
In simplicity of life
In stewardship of creation
In the healing of the world
In stream of God's Spirit

In solidarity with all
In sharing with others
In love of Trinity.

SOCIAL JUSTICE AND POLITICS

THE ARC OF THE MORAL UNIVERSE IS LONG, BUT IT
BENDS TOWARDS JUSTICE... LET NO ONE ATTEMPT
WITH SMALL GIFTS OF CHARITY TO EXEMPT HIMSELF
FROM THE GREAT DUTIES IMPOSED BY JUSTICE.

PIUS II

I know missional Christians from three schools of thought. The first believe that Christians should not waste time on justice because Jesus might return tomorrow, so our priority must be to save souls. The second believe that God is by nature a God of justice, so justice must take priority over evangelism. The third believe that from Christ's infinite compassion flows evangelism through his right arm and justice through his left arm: they are indivisible. Mike Frost helpfully points out that evangelism and social involvement are so entwined that you can't unravel them. They are both equally important and necessary expressions of alerting people to the reign of God. 'We feed the hungry because in the world to come there will be no such thing as starvation. We share Christ because in the world to come there will be no such thing as unbelief.'[94] Aidan modelled this third approach.

King Oswald humbly and willingly, in all things, gave ear to Aidan's admonitions. Once, he invited guests to an Easter celebration at the royal headquarters at Bamburgh. He asked

Bishop Aidan to preside at the Eucharist in the church. This was followed by a splendid banquet. Dainties were placed on silver dishes.

Oswald, it seems, was the first Saxon king to appoint a member of staff to look after the needs of the poor. Soon after the banquet began, this officer informed the king that a crowd of hungry people were outside, begging for food. The king, in a gesture of extravagant generosity, ordered him to take all the starters to the hungry people. Then he ordered that the silver plates be cut into small pieces, and that each hungry person should be given a small piece of silver that would enable them to buy food. Aidan was so moved by this that he held up the king's arm and made a prophecy. 'The arm that has given food to the poor with such compassion shall never perish,' he said. Down the centuries, people have recalled both this story and Aidan's prophecy, for when the tyrant Penda killed Oswald and dismembered his body, a loyal warrior retrieved that arm. It was placed in a casket in Bamburgh church.

This story features care for the poor and prophecy during a respite from evangelistic tours. It is said that the Church of England symbolically keeps alive this ethos when its head layperson, the monarch, gives silver coins to deserving charity workers at a cathedral on the Thursday before Easter (Maundy Thursday) and that this Maundy Service owes its origin to the story of Oswald.

Christians from the 'evangelism only' school say, 'All you need is Jesus.' 'Yes, but you need Jesus on his terms, not yours,' is one reply, and Jesus calls us to tend the 'vineyard' of planet earth (Matthew 21:33–41). The only example he gives of someone who enters God's kingdom is the one who gives to a needy person (Matthew 25:31–40). Jesus inspired the apostle Paul to teach that, in Christ, 'there is no longer slave or free' (Galatians 3:28).

KINGDOM POLITICS

Jesus used a political term to describe his mission—a 'kingdom'. As Marcus Borg has pointed out, Jesus could have spoken of the people of God or the community of God or the family of God, but instead he spoke of the kingdom of God.[95] Jesus' hearers knew about the subkingdom of Herod and the kingdom of Rome. The kingdom of God is a political metaphor. It is about God in this world. The Jews looked to a messiah who would overthrow the Roman occupiers and install their own kingdom of justice.

The kingdom of God is about God, in contrast to the egocentric world that most people rely on, and in contrast to the egocentric faith that many Christians have constructed. Jesus urges his followers to pray, 'Your kingdom come on earth.' The kingdom of God stands in contrast to the ancient domination system ('The rulers of the Gentiles lord it over them... but whoever wishes to be great among you must be your servant', Matthew 20:25–26). The kingdom of God is what life would be like on earth if God were king and the rulers of this world cooperated. It is about justice, mercy and peace. It is about relationship: 'Our Father... your kingdom come.' This is what Jesus likened to the effect of yeast in dough—transformation.

The evangelism-only school not only misses what Jesus is about; it misses an opportunity to win a new generation who want to commit to a radical vision of justice. It fails to win young people who realise that individual*ism* (as distinct from individual*ity*) is a sin. The narrative fed to the ISIL (Islamic State) recruits by social media is that existing societies are godless, so they must be overthrown and replaced by a Caliphate that enforces God's laws as taught by their (perverted) form of Islam. They feel that a campaign to replace the existing political order with a Caliphate that establishes God's kingdom on earth is worth fighting and dying for. This puts Western evangelists on the back foot because they fail to realise that they are perceived as part of a godless, Muslim-killing empire. It puts politicians on the back foot because they should be criticising the selfishness of their society as well as honouring its merits. It also fails to impress mainstream Muslims who believe that God wants a world community of justice—*Ummah*.

WHO IS AT YOUR TABLE?

In Aidan's vision of society, everyone had a relationship of respect with others. That is why he took time to be with both the marginalised and the rulers. It is why he challenged unjust landowners. It is why no person had more possessions than another in his monasteries. This reflects biblical teaching. The Brehon Laws of the Irish, which St Patrick and his successors helped to shape, were steeped in the Old Testament social justice laws.

The New Testament often uses the Greek word *oikos*, which means 'house'. Both the church and the world are called *oikos*. From it we derive our words 'economy' and 'ecumenism'. A common home may have many rooms and various levels, but in it everyone can connect with the others. If the gap between rich and poor in a society is such that there is no touching point, that society is sick. Without a feeling of belonging, trust erodes, unhappiness increases and violence breaks out. This also applies locally. 'Sink' housing estates with generations of unemployed people increase, as do gang warfare, drug dependency and crime.

Aidan wanted a society in which everyone was, so to speak, in the same household. That is a realisable aim for our time. For example, those who apply to become Members of Parliament should be expected to have on their CV a period spent working with the most deprived.

At Urban Seed's Credo Café in the centre of Melbourne, all are welcome at the table. Housed in the Collins Street Baptist Church, a group of Christians live together and offer hospitality to the marginalised at the back door leading off a laneway, while inviting the prestigious front-door neighbours to experience a different form of hospitality also. Leaders in business are invited to come and share food with the city's marginalised people. They are not there to 'help' the poor by cooking at a soup kitchen, but experience a relational conversation. Many merchant bankers have been surprised to hear that they went to the same prestigious school as the man hidden under an unwashed beard who has acquired a mental illness and been shunned by society. Relationships are further created by a programme called 'Laneway Cricket', where the corporate sector can come together with homeless people and play a similar format to indoor cricket, using Melbourne's iconic laneways. The concept aims to create a safer city by bringing together the diverse city inhabitants to play on the same team, thus breaking down stereotypes and creating greater understanding.

In their book *The Spirit Level: Why equality is better for everyone*, Richard Wilkinson and Kate Pickett use years of research from eight rich countries to provide hard evidence that almost everything—from life expectancy to mental illness, violence to illiteracy—is affected not by how wealthy a rich society is, but by how equal it is.[96] A list of problems that increase in more unequal societies includes falling levels of trust, mental illness (including drug and alcohol addiction), low life expectancy and infant mortality, obesity, low educational performance, teenage births, homicides, imprisonment rates and social mobility. In such countries, health and well-being are no longer a common experience.

The charity Redeeming Our Communities, founded in 2004 by Debra Green OBE, equips Christians who seek to work with people of goodwill for 'the welfare of the city' (Jeremiah 29:7). In her book *ROC Your World: Changing communities for good*, Green suggests that the redeeming of our communities stems from four principles:

- Belief that God has a heart for this broken world.
- Belief that God has placed resources within people and institutions in an area, however neglected it is. These resources can be drawn out and the people can be empowered.
- Belief in the value of Christians becoming partners with people of good will. Jesus said, 'Whoever is not against you is for you' (Luke 9:50).
- Belief that the imaginative prayer of Christian partners can open up fresh inspirations for working together for good, renewing areas of neglect and repairing bad relationships.[97]

MODERN SLAVERY

Slavery was part of the fabric of society in the New Testament period of the Roman Empire, and it continued in Anglo-Saxon Britain. Saxon warriors had affairs with indigenous Celtic Britons and dumped the children at slave markets, some of whom were transported to Rome. There, the future Pope Gregory, when he was Rome's Prefect, famously said of them, 'Not Angles but angels.' Aidan did something about it.

Rich landowners gave Aidan donations, which he passed on to the poor. Sometimes he went to a market and purchased freedom for a slave. Aidan, with his shepherd heart, took an interest in these freed slaves and asked what they hoped to do with their liberty. Some were given jobs in the fields or the kitchens of his monastic villages, or even, if they had an aptitude for study, a place in a school. Some former slaves became priests.

Despite William Wilberforce's achievement in abolishing the slave trade in the British Empire, human slavery has increased to an unprecedented 29 million. In 2013, Pope Francis and Archbishop Justin Welby launched the Global Freedom Network to eradicate modern slavery. The following year, Anglican, Catholic, Orthodox, Muslim, Hindu and Jewish leaders signed a joint Declaration Against Modern Slavery. The organisation aims to get regulations agreed that stop the supply chain, offer alternatives to those who 'lose' their slave labour, and provide care for victims.

Black theologian Robert Beckford presented one of a series of six TV programmes on the history of Christianity. His episode focused on Aidan's mission and Lindisfarne. Beckford said that although he was a committed Christian, he had always been ambivalent because his forebears received the gospel through slave owners. Now, at last, he had discovered a model of Christianity, that preceded the British Empire's slave trade, in which he could believe wholeheartedly.

Aidan spoke truth to power. When wealthy people mistreated their employees or neighbours, Aidan rebuked them, even though they tried to soften him up with large donations. People he mentored also stood up to people in high places who mistreated others or did wrong things. Hilda sent an emissary to Rome to put the case for one of her former ordinands who was being mistreated by the prelate Wilfred. Cedd rebuked the East Saxons' king for stealing another's wife.

CHURCH AND STATE

This raises the question of what should be the relationship between church and state. The church and the state can relate to one another in one of four ways.

- The church rules. Theocracy has been tried. It is always a disaster, because power corrupts.
- The state rules, and church and religions are relegated to private life. This is an abdication by the church and makes a mockery of Jesus' call to bring God's kingdom on earth.
- There is a separation of powers. Some Protestant nations have followed this route. Critics claim that the separation of

church and state in Germany allowed Hitler to control the soul and body of Germany, because the overground church refused to oppose him.

• Church and state are good, though challenging, neighbours.

Revd James F. Cassidy, of St Paul's Minnesota, wrote of the early Irish monastic church that it 'never became, as in other lands, by turns the servant, the ally, or the master of the State. It was the companion of the people, and an important element in the national life.'[98] Columba was steeped in politics. If he had not become a monk, he might have become High King of Ireland. As abbot of Iona, he chose and anointed Aidan McGabran as king of Dalriada—thought to be the first king in Europe anointed by a Christian leader.

Aidan and Oswald give us a working model of how a church leader and a state ruler can work together for the communal well-being, make strategic alliances and sponsor a host of good projects. Oswald's successor, the more nominal Christian Oswy, along with his Romanised Queen Enfleda, required 'their' bishop to be ever more often at court as the church grew and consultations multiplied. Aidan did not, however, allow his times alone with God to be squeezed out. He had a cell constructed on the outskirts of the royal compound at Bamburgh, where he sometimes lived and prayed. From it he would walk out to his mission journeys. His legendary discretion enabled him to 'do business' with a ruler who could use the church for his own ends but who recognised that the church was a force to be reckoned with: with people like Aidan around, God could not be mocked. When Northumbria split again into two subkingdoms, Aidan spent more time at York, where the Christlike King Oswin ruled over the southern kingdom of Deira. They no doubt planned to establish new faith communities, and Oswin gave Aidan his best royal horse, despite Aidan's habit of walking everywhere, because of the increased duties of mission and maintenance.

Aidan's relationship with Oswy's Queen Enfleda was not easy. About 648, she sponsored a brilliant student named Wilfred, who came to the school at Lindisfarne as an attendant to an unwell nobleman. Wilfred, like his sponsor, loved all things Roman and despised the humble Irish ways. He made his views known on every occasion. The simplicity and equality of regard that Aidan had inculcated at Lindisfarne came under threat. Yet such was Aidan's discretion that he retained a working relationship with the queen.

Poverty is about breakdown of relationships, not just about lack of material things. Aidan realised that projects including Oswy's donations of lands for new monasteries would not fulfil God's purposes unless they were based on relationship. Patrick Dodson, a respected Australian indigenous leader, told *The Sunday Age*, 'We've got to get away from just thinking about programs and policy and start thinking in terms of relationships.'[99] Eminent Australian and revered indigenous leader Pastor Sir Doug Nicholls said in a historically significant sermon:

> *I want to suggest three things why you should bother about the Aborigines. First, we belong to the great family of God and he has made out of one blood all nations of men. Secondly... we're a part of the great British Commonwealth of Nations. And thirdly, we want to walk with you, we don't wish to walk alone.*[100]

The Community of Aidan and Hilda's Way of Life states:

> *Our mission also includes speaking out for the poor, the powerless and those unjustly treated in our society and to minister to and with them as God directs... Celtic evangelists worked hand in hand with those in authority to bring regions and kingdoms under the rule of God, and to open doors to the Gospel. We seek to dialogue and work with people of good will in places of authority and influence so that our lands may be led by God, and become healed lands of the glorious Trinity.*[101]

Members of some churches feel discouraged from reaching out in this spirit because their church is such a poor model. These words of Pope Francis may encourage them: 'It is better to have a Church that is wounded but out in the streets than a Church that is sick because it is closed in on itself.'[102]

President Carter's National Security Advisor, Zbigniew Brzezinski, thought that world peace was possible if there was effective consensus regarding shared sacrifices as well as voluntary cooperation, but 'world peace' imposed by a dominant power, assisted by a few partners, was unlikely. The Oswald–Aidan partnership took the former approach. Oswald not only made alliances with neighbours and former enemies; he developed personal friendships. He was godfather at the baptism of the king of the West Saxons. Their vision that a peace between brother and sister kingdoms throughout Britain would hold sway was thwarted by the remaining dominant pagan kingdom of Mercia, whose King Penda slew Oswald. Nonetheless, Oswald and Aidan made a huge advance in providing a model of peace between peoples. They united four previously warring races.

The struggle between good and evil raged within Anglo-Saxon kingdoms and continent-wide empires, and rages now in today's even larger capitalist empire. The free market, when it has a framework of honest, responsible family, work and social units, has brought untold benefits; but when it is commandeered by monopolies, banks and governments for purposes of greed and power, it succumbs to evil. Company law needs to be changed. Shareholders should be required to make profit not only in cash that goes to themselves but in benefits to the environment and local citizens. Locals and employees should have the right to propose socially responsible policies, as Aidan used his right to challenge landowners who abused their power. Free information enables evils to be exposed and ways of creating the common good to be promoted. This offers unprecedented opportunities to bring God's kingdom on earth. Aidan's is a model whose time has come.

A world organised for individual self-interest does not hold the allegiance of those who are crushed by that self-interest, or of those who feel, deep down, that there must be an alternative basis (whether they call it 'goodness' or 'God'). On the other hand, politicians who condemn capitalism's evils without facing the reality of what it takes to create safe, clean streets, with houses and basic amenities for all, are also guilty of falsehood. Effective missioners thank God for capitalism's blessings and cooperate with God to clean up its sins.

Many thousands of young people from over 90 countries have been sucked into the military campaign to create a Caliphate in the name of God. Goodness soon becomes a victim of hate. Yet these young people have found no more compelling narrative to believe in. The answer is not to say that all things Western are good. It raises the same question about our moral authenticity that T.S. Eliot raised at a dark time in 1938, when he asked if 'our society, which had always been so assured of its superiority and rectitude, so confident of its unexamined premises' was 'assembled round anything more permanent than a congeries of banks, insurance companies and industries, and had it any beliefs more essential than a belief in compound interest and the maintenance of dividends'.[103]

There is an alternative narrative. The message we need to communicate to false Islamist military Jihadists is this. Our countries have good and bad values. Good values include respect for people of all races and genders and income, and for law and order, freedom of conscience, the right to marry a person of one's choice, and freedom of movement, speech and vote. Bad values include disrespect for religion, prophets, the poor and the human body, and economic exploitation of poor countries and the earth. We call on everyone to join a never-ending struggle to overcome evil with good, starting with ourselves.

The sense of the sacred has atrophied even where religious centres are full. The spectres of greed and power reign where there is no God. ISIS mobilises resentment and turns it into killing. Yet people harbour longings for belonging as well as for power and plenty. Rising above a sense of victimhood, we mobilise longing and turn it into community.

Diffusion of power is essential in today's world, but only relationships of trust can hold that diffusion together. The church must model this trust. The flowerpot model of leadership is needed in the church. The normal model is a pyramid, but if you turn a pyramid upside down, you get a flowerpot. The leaders are now at the bottom, nourishing and upholding the members. A strong person can 'do' relief work, education and confrontation, but only together can we do transformation.

The United Nations, in its 1996 Habitat Agenda, calls for 'just cities': 'Equitable human settlements are those in which all people without discrimination of any kind… have equal access to housing, infrastructure, health services, adequate food and water, education and open spaces.' The church is called to be the conscience of politics and the soul of a nation.

REFLECTION

I imagine Aidan explaining to those new recruits to the monastic school whose parents were wealthy landowners that in their new community no one owned more than anyone else: they shared all things in common, and there was no privileged class. I imagine him rejoicing when the rich gave their food to the poor, and when he was able to use donations to purchase the freedom of a slave. What actions for global or local justice does or should your faith community take?

I imagine Aidan in think-tanks with King Oswald, planning how to develop and sustain a commonwealth of once-hostile peoples from four races, knit together in the fellowship of the gospel for the common good. What steps can your faith community take to knit together a fellowship of groups of different ethnic, social or theological backgrounds?

The crisis of our time is the failure of state socialism (under Hitler), communism (under Stalin) and capitalism to create a world family free from poverty, prejudice, abuse and disrespect. Think through criteria for the common good—for example, in Catholic social teaching. How can you put flesh on it?

Ideologies such as ISIL, who recruit young people from many countries in search of a purpose, are not defeated by military means, or by politics, if it is merely the art of managing selfish electorates. Only a better idea, that is lived and modelled, can win over misguided would-be martyrs. So many political leaders on the Right overlook the sins of capitalism; so many on the Left overlook what it takes to maintain a responsible society. These words should be etched in the job descriptions of every person employed in public services: 'Put yourselves in the shoes of those you serve.' Capitalists need to condemn producers who laud the free market yet create a monopoly in order to exact extortionate prices. Former empires such as Britain need to admit to sins such as the slave trade and ethnic massacres, as well as to celebrate what was good. Sacred rage, born of impotence, now has a vehicle. We need to offer a better vehicle, a tougher challenge, a more lasting outcome.

Draw up a missionary manifesto that can win over a new generation who are sick of the world as it is. It might go something like this:

Lay down your lives for a world led by God. Change the world not from the outside but from the inside. Be a partner in the unfolding purposes of God, for ever at work in ourselves and the world. The free money market enables needed goods to be created, adapted and distributed, but the sins of capitalism violate God, justice and the poor. The answer is not to destroy one tyranny, even in the name of God. That will be replaced by another tyranny, because power corrupts. The answer is to engage in a ceaseless war against evils in ourselves and in other people, and to hand over our lives to the source of all good, the all-compassionate one who will show us how to transform evil into good. Jesus, the sinless one, the prophet of the resurrection, is appearing to many people in dreams, experiences and scriptures. He is forming a worldwide force of non-violent volunteers to bring in God's kingdom on earth through transformation. Join us.

May the wealth and work of the world be available to all
and for the exploitation of none.
May employers, shareholders and employees be like fingers on
your hand.

Awaken leaders who, rising above ambition,
free from the bondage of fear,
work for a prejudice-free, hate-free world
where poor and rich are friends
and a thousand flowers bloom.
Give us that dynamic which calls out and combines
the moral and spiritual responsibility of individuals
for their immediate sphere of action.
May our foreign policy be
to earn the trust and gratitude of our neighbours.
May each land find its destiny in your will.
May we seek the common good
and live as fellow citizens of your eternal kingdom.

LIVING EPITAPH

An epitaph values a person's life and legacy. On both counts, Aidan shines.

The scholar J.B. Lightfoot, Bishop of Durham (d.1889), struggled to encapsulate the roles of Augustine of Canterbury and Aidan of Lindisfarne. In the end he concluded that Augustine was the apostle of Kent, while Aidan was the apostle of the English,[104] but even that evaluation falls short. I led a workshop at Scotland's Clan Gathering entitled 'Aidan: the greatest Scot still waiting to be discovered'.[105] Aidan features along with other saints, such as Ninian, Mungo and Columba, in Scotland's National Portrait Gallery. The Irish, known as Scotti, who colonised places such as Dalriada (Argyll), spread out from there and eventually gave their name to Scotland. Aidan was an Irish Scot, and the Northumbria he evangelised included Irish Scots, Welsh-speaking Britons and Picts as well as English.

King Oswald, with the English nation which he governed, being instructed by the teaching of Aidan, not only learned to hope for a heavenly kingdom unknown to his fathers, but also obtained of the one God, Who made heaven and earth, a greater earthly kingdom than any of his ancestors. In brief, he brought under his dominion all the nations and provinces of Britain, which are divided into four languages, to wit, those of the Britons, the Picts, the Scots, and the English. Though raised to that height of regal power, wonderful to relate, he was always humble, kind, and generous to the poor and to strangers. (EH 3.6)

As enthusiasm grows for more autonomy for Scotland, Wales, Northern Ireland and England, some have urged that the United Kingdom as a whole, not just its constituent lands, should have its patron saint. National newspapers have carried articles putting forward Aidan as an ideal candidate.[106] Born in Ireland, trained in Scotland, a missionary bishop in England whose oversight extended to Welsh-speaking Britons—who else represents such unity in diversity?

Aidan transcends nationalism. Christians who throw obvious idols out of the front door can allow the idol of nationalism in through the back door. Aidan, like so many of the Irish 'pilgrims for the love of God', selflessly laid down his life for a neighbouring people in sacrificial mission. There is a vital role for Churches Together in Britain and Ireland in making real a heart-union of these peoples; leadership in the spirit of Aidan can make a difference. Countries anywhere may reach their full flower if, freed from bitterness, victimhood and false self-sufficiency, they embrace the Aidan spirit, which seeks to make other peoples great.

Aidan's approach to mission is universal. He used all means—countryside, community and court—to bring the gospel to new peoples. He took pastorally caring missioners to the people's doorsteps. He established models of God's kingdom in the monastic communities. He befriended and counselled those in the corridors of power who serviced or visited the royal centres.

Even more significant for the longer-term mission, he trained and sent disciples whose influence, directly or indirectly, continued long after his death. Years after Lindisfarne's Irish monks departed in 664, Aidan's English disciples continued to plant churches, mentor rulers (Cedd among the East Saxons, Cynebil in Deira) and model Christlike lives. The monasteries listed in Chapter 5 continued their work.

The successors of Aidan, Finan and Colman, both monks of Iona, extended the mission further. Under Finan, after the pagan King Penda of Mercia was slain, Oswy's son Alchfrid and daughter Alchfled made alliance with Penda's daughter Cuniburh and his son Peada, whom Finan baptised. Cuniburgh, also known as Kynesburgh, is said to have founded a monastery on the site of St Kynesburgh's church, Castor, by the Roman fort at Peterborough. In 656, Finan consecrated the Lindisfarne monk Diuma to be bishop of Mercia (the English Midlands), and his three successors were consecrated by Irish bishops.

Even Colman's successor, Tudor, had been consecrated in the south of Ireland. His quick death by plague and the consecration of Wilfred in 664 as bishop in Northumbria led to the revival of the see of York, yet Aidan's influence still could not be quenched. The monks who remained at Lindisfarne were placed, by special request of Colman, under the care of Eata, abbot of Melrose and one of Aidan's first English pupils. Subsequently, Alchfrid put him in charge of Ripon, to which he brought a colony of monks from Melrose, including Cuthbert. Cuthbert succeeded Boisil at Melrose before being transferred to Lindisfarne. After Wilfred was expelled, Theodore, the Archbishop of Canterbury, divided Northumbria into three dioceses and consecrated three bishops at York. Eata had oversight of Bernicia, his see covering both Hexham and Lindisfarne, until these areas were separated and Cuthbert became the great missionary bishop of Lindisfarne. From Whitby emerged five missionary and healing bishops trained by Hilda.

Brother Damian (Vicar of St Mary's Lindisfarne from 2003 to 2010), speaking at a pilgrimage to St Cedd's foundation at Bradwell-on-Sea in 2006, said:

Celtic monks from Ireland and Iona only lived on Lindisfarne for 29 years. The boys Cedd and Chad were English pupils in our school with their two brothers, and Aidan taught them to journey with a vision—which they did with outstanding zeal, godly determination and singleness of mind. Mission was their fuel for the journeys, the love of Christ and the embracing of a gospel life, to be accepted, shared and enjoyed, following the traditions of their fathers, Patrick, Ninian and Columba.

The influence of Aidan's Irish mission even travelled overseas, albeit as a byproduct of Viking invasion. Recent archaeological research has revealed that along the western coast of Norway, near Stavanger, are signs of Christianity dating from 200 years before the top-down missions that used to be thought the first in Norway. The implication is that slaves and women brought from Aidan's Northumbria spread the faith from the ground up. 'There is a different spirit in that part of Norway,' a Norwegian immigrant said to me. 'It is more gentle and there is a greater sense of community.' If Aidan was like a stone thrown into a pond, these were some of the far-reaching ripples.

It is true that Aidan's beloved Lindisfarne was the first place in Britain that the Vikings ransacked; and that after that, Benedictines, foreigners who behaved like feudal lords, built a priory next to the church that would contribute to a long-lasting wounded memory. Yet it was from Lindisfarne's scriptorium, recovered after the Synod of Whitby setback, that the Lindisfarne Gospels and other fragments that survived pillage, such as the manuscript now known as the Durham Gospels, heralded a golden age that lit up Europe's Dark Age. The Lindisfarne Gospels, described by *The Sunday Times* as 'the book that made Britain', drew its exquisite artistry from Irish, Egyptian and oriental sources, as well as from Rome, Byzantium and the Anglo-Saxons themselves. It became, as some scholars argue, a kind of first manifesto of a truly Anglo-Celtic, English-speaking church.[107]

After the Viking invasions, the Lindisfarne monks relocated to Chester-le-Street, and married monks formed a Community of St Cuthbert to guard Cuthbert's shrine at the site that is now Durham Cathedral. In 995, Bishop Edmund formed the Durham bishopric, but, according to Alfred Webb's *Compendium of Irish*

Biography, Aidan was regarded as the first in its line of bishops.[108] Glastonbury monks obtained some supposed relics of Aidan. Through their influence, Aidan's feast appears in the early Wessex calendars, which provide the main evidence for his cult after the age of Bede. His feast day is on 31 August.

Aidan's Lindisfarne was described by Alcuin, adviser to the Holy Roman Emperor Charlemagne, as 'the most holy place in England', and, because Cuthbert's original shrine there drew more pilgrims than almost any other place, an English king decreed that it should be known as Holy Island. In recent decades, pilgrimage has revived. Those who walk the 63-mile St Cuthbert's Way from Melrose, and the longer St Oswald's Way from Hexham, finish at Lindisfarne.

Now, a yet longer route is being named St Aidan's Way. For some, this starts on a section of the West Highland Way from the shores of Loch Lomond. It follows the John Muir nature walk that stretches from Helensbrough in the Trossachs to Linton, south of Haddington.[109] Then people walk south, more or less along the coast, to Holy Island. Aberlady Conservation and History Society are convinced that Aidan stopped at Aberlady, a little south of Edinburgh, on his way to Lindisfarne. Their interpretation plaques in the Church of Scotland churchyard that overlook the Firth of Forth provide a fine picture of Aidan and his twelve missionary monks landing there. They also name a route from there to Lindisfarne St Aidan's Way, which they believe became a pilgrimage route in the eighth century. The route goes through Abbey St Bathan's, which is named after an abbot of Iona.[110]

Aidan is formally recognised as a saint by the Anglican, Orthodox and Roman Catholic branches of the church, and informally as one of the brightest of 'the cloud of witnesses' (Hebrews 12:1) by many more. He may be seen as a sign of unity in the sense that he straddles the divisions created at the time of the Reformation. I live on the Holy Island of Lindisfarne and am occasionally invited to preside at a Eucharist at St Mary's

Church. This church is on the site of Aidan's original wooden church. Its list of parish clergy reaches back to the early bishops whose see was here, starting with Aidan. In this church, pilgrims light candles or pray before icons of Mary, Aidan and Cuthbert. A visitor, seeing all this, asked me, 'Are you Protestant or Catholic?' I replied, 'I was ordained into the one, holy, catholic and apostolic church at the cathedral in Lichfield, founded in the seventh century by Aidan's disciple Chad.'

A member of The Community of Aidan and Hilda asked one of the founders why they had chosen Aidan, and not Cuthbert, for their name. He replied:

Aidan pioneered it all; Cuthbert came on his back.

Aidan was little known; Cuthbert was a celebrity.

Aidan did cross-cultural indigenous mission; Cuthbert consolidated.

Aidan gave his life for another people; Cuthbert gave his life for his own people.

Aidan walked among the people; Cuthbert rode among them.

Aidan gave all money to the poor; Cuthbert accepted many estates.

Aidan introduced Christian spiritual foster mothers to a new people; Cuthbert had one of them.

Aidan introduced soul friends to the English; Cuthbert was one.

Aidan established the first of many monastic 'villages of God'; Cuthbert was formed in them.

Aidan's body decayed and is not entombed in a famous shrine; Cuthbert's body did not decay in his superior coffin and he is entombed in a prestigious cathedral.

Islands played a significant part in Aidan's life—Scattery (perhaps), Iona and Lindisfarne. The cricketer Conrad Hunt once said to me, 'Islands are God's strategy for continents.' They keep at bay the shouting rush of the mainland and provide space where laboratories of the Holy Spirit may do their work—although hell as well as heaven can get its way. Did Aidan realise, when he chose a tidal island of retreat and outreach, that it could become a symbol of a way of life, as this prayer from the Northumbria Community suggests?

Leave me alone with God as much as may be.
As the tide draws the waters close upon the shore,
make me an island,
set apart, alone with you, God, holy to you.
Then with the turning of the tide
prepare me to carry your presence to the busy world beyond,
the world that rushes in on me,
till the waters come again and fold me back to you.

Visitors to Lindisfarne who embrace its godly rhythms often say, 'I wish we could take the island back with us.' We say, 'You can. Make God your island.'

Lord, you are my island,
in your bosom I nest.
You are the calm of the sea,
in that peace I rest.
You are the waves on the shore's glistening stones,
their sound is my hymn.
You are the song of the birds,
their tune I sing.
You are the sea breaking on rock,
I praise you with the swell.
You are the ocean that laps my being,
in you I dwell.

The famous 18th-century diarist Samuel Johnson exclaimed, 'Oh to God that someone would come forward and rebuild [the monastic ruins of Lindisfarne], that once again they may send forth labourers, filled with the holy enthusiasm of St Aidan, into the wide mission field.' Perchance Aidan's memorial is best served not by rebuilding ruins, but in building for future generations. The meek shall inherit the earth—multitudes worldwide who are rooted and grounded in the Gospels' way of life that he so utterly lived.

AIDAN'S PLACE OF RESURRECTION

Oswy declared war on Oswin in a bid to recolonise Deira. Oswin at first raised an army to combat Oswy's planned attack upon them, but, when he realised that his much smaller number of warriors could not win, he sued for peace rather than cause their death. Oswy agreed and Oswin retired to the house of his friend Hunwald, accompanied only by his faithful warrior Tondhere. Hunwald betrayed him, no doubt seduced by a bribe from Oswy, who had the two refugees killed by his own commander. This place, Ingethlingum, is now called Gilling. In an attempt to make atonement for this crime, Queen Enfleda had a monastery built there where prayers were offered daily for the two kings.

Perhaps the shock of this betrayal caused Aidan to have a stroke or heart attack. They could not move him from his little church at Bamburgh, so they erected a tent around him. He breathed his last leaning against a buttress that was on the outside of the church to strengthen the wall. He died in the 17th year of his mission, after dark on 31 August 651. They took his body to Lindisfarne and buried him in the brothers' cemetery. Later, his bones were placed on the right side of the altar in the larger, stone church that replaced his humble church of wood.

Yet Bamburgh also became a shrine to Aidan.

Some years after his death the tyrant Penda burned down the royal garrison. But the buttress against which Aidan had been leaning when he died, could not be consumed by the fire which devoured all about it. This miracle being noised abroad, the church was soon rebuilt in the same place, and that same

*buttress was set up on the outside, as it had been before, to
strengthen the wall. It happened again, sometime after, that the
village and likewise the church were carelessly burned down the
second time. Then again, the fire could not touch the buttress;
and, miraculously, though the fire broke through the very holes
of the nails wherewith it was fixed to the building, yet it could do
no hurt to the buttress itself. When therefore the church was built
there the third time, they did not, as before, place that buttress
on the outside as a support of the building, but within the church,
as a memorial of the miracle; where the people coming in might
kneel, and implore the Divine mercy. And it is well known that
since then many have found grace and been healed in that same
place, as also that by means of splinters cut off from the buttress,
and put into water, many more have obtained a remedy for their
own infirmities and those of their friends. (EH 3.17)*

That buttress, according to tradition, is now in the rafters above
the font at Bamburgh's St Aidan's Church.

When the Irish monks and 30 Saxon monks departed from
Lindisfarne after the 664 Synod of Whitby, they took some of
Aidan's bones with them. Perhaps a bone was left on Iona, where
they stayed for a short time. Their leader, Bishop Colman, interred
Aidan's bones in the sacristy of the monastery they founded on the
island of Innisboffin, and the Saxons, when they established their
separate monastery on the mainland at Mayo, perhaps took a bone
there, too. When the Vikings invaded Lindisfarne, monks walked
for years with Cuthbert's coffin, which contained one of Aidan's
relics, until it was enshrined at Durham. Over the centuries,
perhaps remaining bones were washed across the ocean.

Many Irish people thought it was essential for a body to be
buried intact, in the deceased person's 'place of resurrection'—
that is, the place to which they were called during their first
earthly life and from which they will be raised at the general
resurrection, to continue their work in the same place. The

resurrection, however, is a new dimension. Is it possible that Aidan's place of resurrection is wherever his spiritual children reside throughout the world and that his widely dispersed bones are a parable of this?

Although Bede criticises Aidan's Irish mission for its views about how to calculate the date of Easter, he is inspired by the manner in which Aidan celebrated this festival of resurrection:

Yet this I approve in him, that in the celebration of his Easter, the object which he had at heart and reverenced and preached was the same as ours, to wit, the redemption of mankind, through the Passion, Resurrection and Ascension into Heaven of the Man Christ Jesus, who is the mediator between God and man. And therefore he always celebrated Easter, not as some falsely imagine, on the fourteenth of the moon, like the Jews, on any day of the week, but on the Lord's day, from the fourteenth to the twentieth of the moon; and this he did from his belief that the Resurrection of our Lord happened on the first day of the week, and for the hope of our resurrection, which also he, with the holy Church, believed would truly happen on that same first day of the week, now called the Lord's day. (EH 3.17)

Aidan and the Irish believed in what the Apostles' Creed calls 'the resurrection of the body' and that God would put them to work on earth: 'You have made them to be a kingdom and priests serving our God, and they will reign on earth' (Revelation 5:10).

Aidan no doubt abandoned himself to God in death as in life. We can only guess at what he sensed about the betrayal and the fruits of his mission. Oswy would convene a synod at Whitby, 13 years after his death, that would replace the Irish people-friendly ethos with a multitude of Roman regulations. Bishop Colman, Aidan's successor at the time of the synod, would obtain (as a special parting favour from Oswy) the appointment of Eata, one of Aidan's twelve English schoolboys, as Abbot of Melrose and then also as Bishop of Lindisfarne. 21st-century Christians would continue to gather at Gilling to pray for the healing of wounded group memory.

At the time Aidan died, an Anglo-Saxon youth named Cuthbert, whose family had become Christians through Aidan's mission, was guarding sheep on the Lammermuir Hills some 40 miles away. He may have been on military duty at the Dunbar garrison, for King Oswy was under threat of attack. While his companions were sleeping, he noticed a long stream of light break through the dark sky and saw what looked like angels descend to earth, receive a spirit of surpassing brightness and escort it to heaven. Cuthbert was so struck by this sight that he yearned to experience spiritual warfare and the happiness that exists among God's mighty ones. He dedicated himself to God with words of praise, and turned his companions' hearts to devotion as he shared his experience with them. The following morning he learned that Bishop Aidan had died at that very time. He immediately handed the sheep back to their owners and determined to enter life-service of Christ in the nearby monastery at Melrose.[111]

Aidan may have died of a broken heart, but rumours of glory, first noted by the young Cuthbert, continue still. In the 21st century he has spiritual children across the world.

On the Sunday of St Aidan's Eve 2015, I looked out on Holy Island's Sanctuary Field, to watch for the pilgrims who had left the church and wended their way along the ancient monastic bounds. Through Skype, I also joined the Community of Aidan and Hilda on the other side of the world, in a liturgy prepared by the group in Buderim, Queensland. Various readers spoke the following words:

We thank you for the life of Aidan, the apostle to the English. We remember the establishing and flowering of the monastic community on Holy Island under Aidan's leadership—a flame which still burns brightly in the English church, including here in the Antipodes.

We are grateful for Aidan's example and way of life which provide waymarks we still follow today. We are grateful for his simple lifestyle and way of walking, and not riding, with the locals. We are grateful for the example of careful listening and humble service to the local people.

I am sorry for the times when I don't follow Aidan's example of simplicity, humility, and regarding all peoples as equal. I am sorry for the times I have ignored and neglected my neighbours who were sick, needy or in distress, especially when I contributed to their distress. I am sorry for the way the Australian church actively participated in the dispossession of the Indigenous people and the subsequent culture of denial of these injustices. I am sorry that in the Middle Ages the British monasteries who were wealthy landowners often exploited and impoverished their tenants. I am sorry for the times when my community and my church are inward-looking and don't follow Aidan's example of caring for the local people.

They then prayed a blessing on Holy Island—islanders, newcomers and visitors—and ended with the words 'May they continue to export Aidan's Way to the ends of the earth.'

AIDAN'S RELEVANCE TO A POST-CHRISTIAN WORLD

It can be argued that although there is much to admire and learn from Aidan, his model of mission has little relevance to a post-Christian Western world. Unlike his, today's world is secular. Two thousand years of organised Christian religion, now subject to relentless scrutiny by the media, have created a need for what Bonhoeffer called 'religionless Christianity'. The free market, not a king, opens or closes doors, and the inherited church is perceived as a problem more than an opportunity. Such criticisms relate to the context but not to the core of mission.

Aidan can inspire us to be indigenous in the sense that we accompany secular people from where they are, understanding their presuppositions. Secular people also have their gods, but they are called by different names, such as money, sex and power. People today do not want a checklist of beliefs that they have to assent to, or a Jesus who has been turned into a celebrity product to be formatted and mass-marketed. They do, deep down, want a way of life that is life-giving, realistic, true, holistic, flexible and endlessly explorable. Aidan modelled such a way of life.

It is true that, under Oswald, Aidan had the mission field to himself in terms of activities organised from the royal centre—but Aidan worked at ground level. At ground level there were, no doubt, diffuse local power games. In my novel *Aidan of Lindisfarne*, an enclave of Welsh-speaking Britons at Brennecatum are totally resistant to the approaches of the Irish mission brothers until an accident (a brother breaks his leg) and a divine inspiration (a festival of St Patrick, who, as a teenage Briton, was captured by Irish pirates in that region) enable a relationship to grow.[112] Certainly, in capitalist countries, some missional pioneers view the land as a marketplace in which it is good to compete: the 'best' mission or church will 'succeed'. What we learn from Aidan is the necessity of relationship—relationship with both overarching and neighbourhood authorities; relationship with other Christian workers so that respect and harmony mark the body of Christ; relationship with people of other faiths and no faith. The Aidan Way is flexible enough to discern situations where it is right to start an experiment; it is relational enough to tend towards community rather than fragmentation.

A poster produced by Australian Aboriginal activists states, 'If you have come to help me, you are wasting my time. But if you have come because your liberation is bound up with mine, then let us work together.' The Aidan Way is relational in this fundamental sense: 'As all die in Adam, so will all be made alive in Christ' (1 Corinthians 15:22).

The assumption that secularism, not religion, is the primary context for contemporary mission may in any case be out of date. Tony Blair has argued in recent speeches that ISIL is now the world's greatest challenge, and that only religion, not politics alone, can answer it. Yet any version of religion that is less holistic and more fragmented than ISIL has little chance. The Aidan Way offers us a route forward.

In what sense? Perhaps the most significant element of Aidan's legacy is that he changed the brutal Anglo-Saxon psyche. A glorious school of poetry expressed this transformation. In this school's greatest poem, 'The Dream of the Rood', Jesus is portrayed as an Anglo-Saxon warrior who leaps lithely upon the cross to save humankind.[113] The poem represents one of the most far-reaching cultural transformations in the history of the world: the sword gives way to the weapon of defenceless love. The message now, as then, is that if we have not done the work of conquering the demons within us, we bring disaster to the world. If we conquer the warmonger inside us, we can bring in a higher form of civilisation.

Carl G. Jung has likened the journey from the false ego-self to the true God-self as the stuff of heroes. By descending into the places of darkness and destruction a hero enables a transformation to take place. The supreme example of this is Jesus Christ descending into Golgotha and hell and enabling a vast transformation at the deepest levels of existence. Aidan's Mission resulted in the power of compassion replacing the power of killing in the popular Dream.

AIDAN THE MAN

What sort of people do we need to become in order to be part of such a dynamic today? A radio tribute to a man who had died described him as 'all gift, no threat'. In a sermon at St Mary's Holy Island on St Aidan's Sunday, Canon Kate Tristram asked how there could be such a man: they are so rare in history. She answered:

> *There was a man who seemed to his friends to be all gift—no threat... Aidan was a volunteer offering to do a job another said was impossible. His gift of himself to Northumbria was a gift for life... There was no guarantee that he would survive. Behind his gift of himself to Northumbria lay a total gift of himself to God, for whatever God willed, whether life or death. We know that he and his monks went out defenceless, to walk the lanes... Taking threats and turning them into gifts could almost have been Aidan's motto... Those who have made giving their aim have surely lived very close to the God who so loved the world that he gave.*

What were the qualities that marked this man who was 'all gift'? We have noted that Bede singles out one word above all others to describe Aidan: discretion. This stems from the Latin *discreti*, from which come our modern words 'discreet' and 'discriminate'. Discretion is the ability to judge and act wisely. Aidan could discriminate between wise and unwise words and courses of action. He could separate that which was of God from that which was not. 'An ounce of discretion is worth a pound of wit,' says the American proverb. 'Honesty doesn't mean you reveal everything you discern and feel. That is why we have the word discretion,' writes Assegid Habtewold in *The 9 Cardinal Building Blocks for Continued Success in Leadership*.[114]

Today the phrase 'emotional intelligence' is used to describe aspects of discretion. How well do we understand and express our own emotional make-up? How well do we understand and relate to that of others? How well do we understand the roots of positive and negative emotions, and the way transitions are best made from one to the other? Discretion is the better part of valour, for valour alone can leave a trail of unforeseen disasters.

Bede says that Aidan's discretion was already evident to the

Iona elders but, as time went on, other virtues also became apparent in him, which Bede heartily admired and loved and wished to preserve for the memory of his readers. They included gentleness, piety, moderation and zeal; a love of peace and charity; continence and humility; 'his mind superior to anger and avarice, and despising pride and vainglory'.

Gentleness, which the apostle Paul lists as one of the nine fruit of the Holy Spirit, is the characteristic needed when exercising discipline (Galatians 6:1), facing opposition (2 Timothy 2:25), and opening ourselves to hearing God's word without pride (James 1:21). Gentleness has soothing qualities such as politeness, kindness and courtesy; yet it has a backbone of steel. The gentle person expresses anger for the right reason and duration and in the right way. Plato considered gentleness to be the cement of society.

Piety is the quality of a devout heart that longs for and refers all things to God. Moderation maximises team achievement and minimises grandiose claims that sidetrack people from being in the centre of God's will. Zeal is the passion that animates a person, night and day, to be alert, give their best and care deeply.

Aidan kept the peace even with antagonists such as Oswy and Oswin, not because he feared to cross their will but because he refused to stoke the fires of ill-will. He could still the storm and remain calm when all around were tempestuous. Charity, or love, showed in his generosity of heart and tender loving care towards people of all backgrounds whom he visited, and in his tears when he observed Oswald, for example, expressing love for the poor through alms.

His continence, or self-control, was forged, I suspect, in inner disciplines that he honed during his vigils. His humility had the strength of the meek who inherit the earth. Aidan was other- not ego-centred.

If Aidan had been ruled by a 'fear or favour' mentality, he would have been in the pocket of the king and his court. If he had been on his high horse or had used donations to advance his own community rather than giving them to the poor, he would have created a 'them and us' perception among the people and damaged the mission.

If he had publicly condemned Queen Enfleda's partisan patronage of his novice monk Wilfred, which undermined the classless society that had marked the Lindisfarne monastic community, he would have pitched the entire mission into conflict. If, in the later years of his ministry, when Northumbria was divided into the two subkingdoms of Bernicia and Deira, he had favoured Oswin, the Christlike king of Deira, over Oswy, the double-minded king of Bernicia, he would have weakened his role as the bishop of all Northumbrians who treated all with equal regard.

One reason why the church seems ineffective in some lands is that it surrounds itself with walls of prejudice and immature behaviour. It pigeonholes its own people and condemns those outside. If it would release people from its judgement, it could empower a multitude. Aidan stood for a prejudice-free approach that offered humble, attentive listening and openness to God in the other person.

Aidan had to learn those lessons before he left Iona. We need to learn the mindset and sensitivities of each player in a situation. An innocent word or action can cause a trail of negativity because it is perceived in the light of the wounded history of a person or group. Corman fell into that trap; Aidan did not.

Aidan's authenticity was as fundamental as his discretion. He dressed in simple woollen clothes and refused to ride a horse, because that would put him physically above the poor, who could not afford horses. Aidan never changed his demeanour, whether at the monastery, at the court or among the poor. He had what we would call 'street cred'. He did not promote the building of impressive churches or give prestige to clergy, as in the Roman tradition, even though he did inspire some of the most beautiful pieces of art known to humankind, such as the

Lindisfarne Gospels. To have authenticity is to do the right thing when no one knows of it.

Aidan was mindful and listened with an open heart. He walked with brothers, unescorted, in a foreign land and memorised and meditated upon the Gospels. He taught his brothers to greet and befriend each person they met, and to listen to their stories and beliefs. Only then did the brothers ask if the new friend would like to hear their own stories and beliefs. Today we call this interfaith dialogue.

Aidan's stature and ability to sustain good relationships held together a church that had incipient splits within it. At the time of the Irish mission to the English, the huge controversy about the date of Easter split churches. Yet Bede writes:

While Aidan lived, this difference about the observance of Easter was patiently tolerated by all people, for they well knew, that though he could not keep Easter contrary to the custom of those who had sent him, yet he industriously laboured to practise the works of faith, piety, and love, according to the custom of all holy people; for which reason he was deservedly beloved by all, even by those who differed in opinion concerning Easter, and was held in veneration... even by the bishops, Honorius of Canterbury, and Felix of the East Angles. (EH 4.25)

Aidan became an example of a man of God who transcended polarisation within the church and established good relationships with leaders across the spectrum.

Rich lessons about leadership reside in the life and work of Aidan. Some emergent mission networks find fault with the historic threefold model of leadership—bishops, presbyters and deacons. They prefer the apostle Paul's reference to five types of leader—apostles, prophets, evangelists, shepherds and teachers (APEST)—in Ephesians 4:11.

I think these represent only a small sample of spiritual callings. Peter Wagner, the Pentecostal author, listed 27 callings mentioned in the New Testament, including hospitality and celibacy. Aidan excelled in each of the APEST roles in different periods of his mission, but he never made a 'career' of them. He prophesied humbly and appropriately, only when the situation called it forth. He was a tender shepherd and a thoughtful teacher, but, as the churches grew, he spent more time at strategic centres such as Lindisfarne, York and Wearmouth. Meanwhile, his disciples shepherded souls in the settlements and churches with similar tenderness, or taught students in the monastic schools.

The maxim 'Delegate everything except leadership itself' was true of Aidan. His calling as bishop was not in contradiction to the other gifts. It was the calling to oversight, the sustaining of a framework conducive to the common good and to relationships that built up everyone as members of the one body of Christ 'until all of us come to the unity of the faith and of the knowledge of the Son of God, to maturity, to the measure of the full stature of Christ' (Ephesians 4:13). His role as bishop was not self-appointed. He submitted to the wisdom of others. This did not diminish his authority but increased it.

We might ask about a synchronicity in timing: Aidan was being prepared for his great life's work during the very years that the prophet Mohammed was receiving revelations, between 610 and 632. A standardised text of these revelations, the Quran, was produced in 650, one year before Aidan's death, while Gospels were being produced in the Irish and English scriptoriums. A chaplain from a Gulf State meditated, while on Lindisfarne, on how different the history of Islam and Christianity might have been if the Prophet had met Christians such as Aidan from Celtic lands. Mohammed met Christians who, he thought, believed in three gods—the Father, the Son and Mary—and, since he knew that idolatry was a sin, he rejected their religion. If he had met the likes of Aidan and his Irish brothers and sisters, he would have known that Christians were people who fell in love with the triune God. The righting of this abhorrent misconception remains an overriding obligation for Christians.

We might also ask, 'What's in a name?' The Irish spelling of Aidan was Aodhan, which is a pet name for Aodh, an Indo-European name meaning 'fire'. Anglicised versions include Aidan, Aiden and Edan, which can be used for females as well as males. Some girls are named Edana, also from the same root. Aed Ruad was a legendary High King of Ireland. Various Irish saints are named Aidan. In recent decades, Aidan has revived as a popular name in North America, and was the most popular boys' name in Canada in 2007. The classic British TV soap *Heartbeat* is set in a Yorkshire village called Aidensfield.

We do not know whether Aidan was named 'Flame' because of his hair colour or his temperament or because the name had some family appeal. We do know that Kathleen Parbury's iconic statue of the saint, completed in 1958 in St Mary's Churchyard, Holy Island, depicts him holding forth a torch of flame. The flame becomes a blazing faith that we are invited to pass on in our time.

A pilgrim knelt at the foot of this sculpture and wrote these words:

Oh Aidan, you had the vision of a population transformed in Christ.
You had the faith to come.
You had the gentleness to win the hearts of king and commoner.
You ministered in power and patience to the sick and dying.
You created teamwork.
Your visits to tell people Good News gave your team a pattern to follow.
You loved the people of the island.
You lived simply and prayed much.
You prepared a mission to the kingdom.
You influenced many to reach others for Christ.
You are Christ for this nation.
You are apostle to this people.

You are in pain that people here are heedless of your Lord.
You will not rest till they are won.
Father, put the mantle of Aidan upon me.

Another pilgrim knelt before Aidan's memorial in Bamburgh church. She heard a voice say, 'Come to me, my daughter, and serve my people here.' She somehow knew that 'here' did not mean Bamburgh: perhaps it meant that she was to learn here to serve Aidan's spiritual children wherever they were.

Simon Reed, a Guardian of the Community of Aidan and Hilda, wrote:

The Celtic Christianity of Aidan and Hilda shows us people with their eyes on the sun and mud on their knees. They are at home in the glory of the ascension and in the darkness of the tomb. They burn with the love of God and bleed in their own bodies with the pains of this world. They live in connection with the scriptures and the Spirit, the saints and the streets, the seasons and the soil.[115]

James Percival, who co-leads the Community of Aidan and Hilda's work in North Wales, gives me permission to include his poem 'You cannot heal'.

You cannot heal a heart
with one that has not been pierced.

You cannot see the Truth
with eyes that have not wept.

You cannot touch a soul
with one that has not known the darkness of night.

You cannot mop a brow
with a cloth that has not bandaged a wound.

You cannot hold a hand
with one not shaped by love.

*You cannot carry a burden
with a back not already broken with a load.*

*You cannot rise
unless you fall;*

*You cannot see
unless you are blind;*

*You cannot live
unless you die;*

*You cannot hold
unless you let go.*

JAMES PERCIVAL, LLANDONNA, ANGLESEY/YNYS MON

This is the basis of authentic mission. This is my epitaph for Aidan.

BIBLIOGRAPHY

David Adam, *Flame in my Heart: St Aidan for today* (Triangle, 1997)

Adomnan of Iona, *Life of St Columba*, trans. and intro. Richard Sharpe (Penguin Classics, 1995)

Leonardo Boff, *Holy Trinity*, Perfect Community (Orbis, 2000)

David Bosch, *Transforming Mission: Paradigm shifts in theology of mission* (Orbis, 1991).

Ian Bradley, *Colonies of Heaven: Celtic models for today's church* (DLT, 2000)

Brother Ramon SSF, *The Heart of Prayer: Finding a time, a place and a way to pray* (Zondervan, 1995)

Michelle P. Brown, *The Lindisfarne Gospels: Society, spirituality and the scribe* (University of Toronto Press, 2003)

Walter Brueggemann, *The Land: Place as gift, promise, and challenge in biblical faith* (Fortress Press, 1977)

Todd Burpo and Sonja Burpo, *Heaven is for Real: A little boy's astounding story of his trip to heaven and back* (Thomas Nelson, 2010)

Gernot Candolini, *Labyrinths: Walking toward the center* (Crossroad, 2003)

Thomas Owen Clancy and Gilbert Markus, *Iona: The earliest poetry of a Celtic monastery* (Edinburgh University Press, 1995)

Richard Coates, Andrew Breeze and David Horovitz, *Celtic Voices, English Places: Studies of the Celtic impact on place-names in England* (Shaun Tyas, 2000).

David Cole, *The Mystic Path of Meditation: Beginning a Christ-centred journey* (Harding House, 2013)

Neil Cole, *Organic Church: Growing faith where life happens* (Jossey-Bass, 2005)

Hugh Connolly, *Irish Penitentials: And the sacrament of penance today* (Four Courts Press, 1994)

Tony Cupit, Ros Gooden and Ken Manley (eds), *From Five Barley Loaves: Australian Baptists in global mission 1864–2010* (Mosaic Press, 2011)

John Drane, *The McDonaldisation of the Church: Spirituality, creativity and the future of the Church* (DLT, 2000)

David Edward, *The Futures of Christianity* (Hodder & Stoughton, 1987)

Eileen Farrelly, *Dadirri: The Spring Within: The spiritual art of the Aboriginal people from Australia's Daly River region* (Terry Knight, 2003)

Richard Fletcher, *The Conversion of Europe: From paganism to Christianity 371–1386* (Fontana, 1988).

Michael Frost and Alan Hirsch, *The Shaping of the Things to Come: Innovation and mission for the 21st-century church* (Hendrickson, 2003)

Hugh Graham, *The Early Irish Monastic Schools: A study of Ireland's contribution to early medieval culture* (BiblioBazaar, 2009)

Debra Green OBE, *ROC Your World: Changing communities for good* (River Publishing, 2014)

Assegid W. Habtewold, *The 9 Cardinal Building Blocks for Continued Success in Leadership* (Success Pathways, 2014)

Andy Harnell and Dan Yarnell, *Forming Multicultural Partnerships: Church planting in a divided society* (Instant Apostle, 2015)

William R. Herzog II, *Parables as Subversive Speech: Jesus as pedagogue of the oppressed* (Westminster John Knox, 1994)

Alan Hirsch, *The Forgotten Ways: Reactivating the missional church* (Brazos, 2009)

Stephanie Hollis, *Anglo-Saxon Women and the Church* (Boydell, 1998)

Irenaeus, *Against Heresies* (Beloved Publishing, 2014)

Philip Jenkins, *The Next Christendom: The coming of global Christianity* (Oxford University Press, 2011)

Ivan Jordan, *Their Way: Towards an indigenous Warlpiri Christianity* (Charles Darwin University Press, 2003)

Ross Langmead, *The Word Made Flesh: Towards an incarnational missiology* (Lanham University Press, 2004)

Alma C. Lightbody, *You're Not the Boss of Me: Discover your authentic self* (iUniverse, 2012)

Stephen Mansfield, *Never Give In: The extraordinary character of Winston Churchill* (Cumberland House, 2002)

H.J. Massingham, *The Tree of Life* (Jon Carpenter, 2003)

Alasdair MacIntyre, *After Virtue* (University of Notre Dame Press, 2007)

Thomas Nolan, *Irish Universities and Culture* (Catholic Truth Society of Ireland, 1914)

Russ Parker, *Healing Wounded History: Reconciling peoples and healing places* (DLT, 2002)

John O'Donovan (trans.), *The Martyrology of Donegal: A calendar of the saints of Ireland* (Forgotten Books, 2015)

John O'Hanlon, *The Lives of the Irish Saints with Special Festivals and Commemorations of Holy Persons Compiled from Calendars, Martyrologies and Various Songs Relating to the Ancient Church History of Ireland*, Vol. 6 (Burns, Oates and Co., 1875) (https://archive.org/details/livesirishsaint00ohagoog)

Uinseann O'Maidin, *The Celtic Monk: Rules and writings of early Irish monks* (Cistercian Studies No. 162) (Cistercian Publications, 1996)

Deirdre O'Sullivan and Robert Young, *The English Heritage Book of Lindisfarne Holy Island* (Batsford, 1995)

Charles Plummer, *Bethada Nádem nÉrenn, Lives of Irish Saints, Vol. 2: Edited from the Original MSS, with Introduction, Translations, Notes, Glossary and Indexes* (Forgotten Books, 2015)

Charles Plummer, *Vitae Sanctae Hiberniae*, Vol. I (BiblioLife, 2009)

Alan J. Roxburgh, *Missional: Joining God in the neighbourhood* (Baker, 2011)

John Sentamu (ed.), *On Rock or Sand? Firm foundations for Britain's future* (SPCK, 2015)

Ray Simpson, *A Pilgrim Way: New Celtic monasticism for everyday people (with study guide)* (Kevin Mayhew, 2014)

Marina Smyth, *Understanding the Universe in Seventh-Century Ireland* (Boydell, 1996)

Paul Sparks, Tim Soerens and Dwight J. Friesen, *The New Parish: How neighborhood churches are transforming mission, discipleship and community* (IVP, 2014)

Bruce Stanley, *Forest Church: A field guide to nature connection for groups and individuals* (Mystic Christ, 2013)

David Tacey, *ReEnchantment: The new Australian spirituality* (HarperCollins Australia, 2000)

A. Hamilton Thompson (ed.), *Bede: His life, times, and writings* (OUP, 1969)

Arnold Joseph Toynbee, *Hellenism: The history of a civilization* (Greenwood Press 1981)

Miroslav Volf, *Exclusion and Embrace: A theological exploration of identity, otherness and reconciliation* (Abingdon, 1996)

Graham Ward, *Cities of God* (Routledge, 2000)

F.E. Warren, *The Liturgy and Ritual of the Celtic Church* (Wipf & Stock, 2008)

Alfred Webb, *Compendium of Irish Biography* (Spalding, 2009)

Richard Wilkinson and Kate Pickett, *The Spirit Level: Why equality is better for everyone* (Penguin, 2010)

NOTES

1 Justin Welby, Archbishop of Canterbury, House of Lords, 26 September 2014

2 Stephen Mansfield, *Never Give In: The extraordinary character of Winston Churchill* (Cumberland House, 2002), p. 190

3 Professor Henry Chadwick, quoted in John Sentamu (ed.), *On Rock or Sand?* (SPCK, 2015)

4 David Edwards, *The Futures of Christianity* (Hodder & Stoughton, 1987)

5 Philip Jenkins, *The Next Christendom: The coming of global Christianity* (Oxford University Press, 2011)

6 Miroslav Volf, *Exclusion and Embrace: A theological exploration of identity, otherness and reconciliation* (Abingdon, 1996), p. 228

7 Michael Frost and Alan Hirsch, *The Shaping of the Things to Come: Innovation and mission for the 21st-century church* (Hendrickson, 2003)

8 David Bosch, *Transforming Mission: Paradigm shifts in theology of mission* (Orbis, 1991)

9 *Mission-Shaped Church* (Church House Publishing, 2004)

10 www.churchgrowthresearch.org.uk/UserFiles/File/Reports/churchgrowthresearch_freshexpressions.pdf

11 See www.freshexpressions.org.uk/news/anglicanresearch

12 See www.freshexpressions.org.uk/news/anglicanresearch

13 John Drane, *The McDonaldisation of the Church: Spirituality, creativity and the future of the Church* (DLT, 2000)

14 Miriam-Rose Ungunmerr-Baumann, in Eileen Farrelly, *Dadirri: The Spring Within: The spiritual art of the Aboriginal people from Australia's Daly River region* (Terry Knight, 2003), p. ix

15   In Farrelly, *Dadirri: The Spring Within*, p. 31

16   Ivan Jordan, *Their Way: Towards an indigenous Warlpiri Christianity* (Charles Darwin University Press, 2003)

17   Michelle P. Brown, *The Lindisfarne Gospels: Society, spirituality and the scribe* (University of Toronto Press, 2003), p. 321

18   Alan Roxburgh, *Missional: Joining God in the neighbourhood* (Baker, 2011), p. 162. Quoted in Andy Harnell and Dan Yarnell, *Forming Multicultural Partnerships: Church planting in a divided society* (Instant Apostle, 2015)

19   Ross Langmead, *The Word Made Flesh: Towards an incarnational missiology* (Lanham University Press of America, 2004)

20   See www.aidanandhilda.us and http://patloughery.com

21   Frank Nathan Daniel Buchman, *Remaking the World: The Speeches of Frank N.D. Buchman* (Blandford, 1961)

22   See www.ucc.ie/celt/published/T201053

23   See, for example, Richard Fletcher, *The Conversion of Europe: From paganism to Christianity 371–1386* (Fontana, 1988)

24   Adapted from Alan Hirsch, *The Forgotten Ways: Reactivating the missional church* (Brazos, 2009)

25   A translation of the Irish *Life* appears in Charles Plummer, *Bethada Nádem nÉrenn*, Vol. II. The most reliable Latin *Life* appears in Plummer, *Vitae Sanctae Hiberniae*, Vol. I

26   Andy Raine and Neil Arnold, Northumbria Community

27   www.vergenetwork.org/2012/01/12/why-you-cant-build-a-church-on-consumers-alan-hirsch

28   The Rule of St Comgall

29   See Brother Ramon SSF, *The Heart of Prayer* (Zondervan, 1995)

30   Ray Simpson, *Soulfriendship: Celtic insights into spiritual mentoring* (Hodder & Stoughton, 1999)

31   Adapted from Ray Simpson, *A Guide for Soul Friends: The art of the spiritual companion* (Kevin Mayhew, 2008)

32   Thomas Nolan, *Irish Universities and Culture* (Catholic Truth Society of Ireland, 1914), p. 11

33   Maurice O'C. Walshe (trans.), *Complete Mystical Works of Meister Eckhart* (Crossroad, 2010)

34   Václav Havel (trans. Paul Wilson), *The Art of the Impossible: Politics as morality in practice* (Alfred A. Knopf, 1997)

35   David Cole, *The Mystic Path of Meditation: Beginning a Christ-centred journey* (Harding House, 2013), p. 24

36   Steve Chalke, *Christianity*, 2013 (www.premierchristianity. com/Featured-Topics/Homosexuality/The-Bible-and-Homosexuality-Part-One

37   Gernot Candolini, *Labyrinths: Walking toward the center* (Crossroad, 2003), quoted in Alma C. Lightbody, *You're Not the Boss of Me: Discover your authentic self* (iUniverse, 2012), p. 73

38   Todd Burpo, *Heaven is for Real: A little boy's astounding story of his trip to heaven and back* (Thomas Nelson, 2010), pp. 71–72

39   H.J. Massingham, *The Tree of Life* (Jon Carpenter, 2003)

40   Adomnan, *Life of Saint Columba*

41   Irenaeus, *Against Heresies* (Kessinger, 2004)

42   Irenaeus, *Proof of the Apostolic Preaching*, 10 (Paulist Press, 1978)

43   Basil of Caesarea, *Hexaemeron* Homily 5 (Catholic University of America Press, 1975)

44   Thomas O Fiach, *Columbanus In His Own Words* (Veritas, 2012)

45   Marina Smyth, *Understanding the Universe in Seventh-Century Ireland* (Boydell, 1996)

46   Russ Parker, *Healing Wounded History: Reconciling peoples and healing places* (DLT, 2002), p. 8

47   From Brent Lyons-Lee and Ray Simpson, *Celtic Spirituality in the Australian Landscape* by (Saint Aidan Press, 2015)

48   Walter Brueggemann, *Journey to the Common Good*
      (Westminster John Knox, 2010)

49   Pope Francis, *Laudato Si: On Care for Our Common Home*
      (Vatican, 2015)

50   Bruce Stanley, *Forest Church: A field guide to nature connection
      for groups and individuals* (Mystic Christ, 2013)

51   William Herzog, *Parables as Subversive Speech: Jesus as
      pedagogue of the oppressed* (Westminster John Knox, 1994)

52   Ched Myers, *The Biblical Vision of Sabbath Economics* (Tell the
      Word, 2001)

53   David Tacey, *ReEnchantment: The new Australian spirituality*
      (HarperCollins Australia, 2000)

54   John O'Donohue, *Anam Cara* (Bantam, 1997)

55   Sabina Flanagan (ed.), *Secrets of God: Writings of Hildegard of
      Bingen* (Shambhala, 1996)

56   Mark Nepo, *Seven Thousand Ways to Listen: Staying close to
      what is sacred* (Simon & Schuster, 2013)

57   Leonardo Boff, *Holy Trinity, Perfect Community* (Orbis, 2000)

58   See Neil Cole, *Organic Church* (Leadership Network, 2005)

59   Richard Coates, Andrew Breeze and David Horovitz, *Celtic
      Voices, English Places: Studies of the Celtic impact on place
      names in England* (Shaun Tyas, 2000)

60   Ian Bradley, *Colonies of Heaven: Celtic models for today's church*
      (DLT, 2000), p. 11

61   Thomas Owen Clancy and Gilbert Markus, *Iona: The earliest
      poetry of a Celtic monastery* (Edinburgh University Press,
      1994), pp. 19–22

62   Adomnan of Iona, *Life of St Columba* (Richard Sharpe, trans.
      and intro.) (Penguin Classics, 1995)

63   'Northumbrian monasticism' in A. Hamilton Thompson,
      Bede: His life, times and writings (OUP, 1969), p. 57

64   D. O'Sullivan and R. Young, *The English Heritage Book of
      Lindisfarne: Holy Island* (Batsford/English Heritage, 2010)

65   F.E. Warren, *Ritual and Liturgy of the Celtic Church* (Boydell, 1987), p. 16

66   Bradley, *Colonies of Heaven*, p. 27

67   Graham Ward, *Cities of God* (Routledge, 2000)

68   For example, Charles Lamb and Rudolph Muller in the early 1900s

69   For Central Place Theory, see https://en.wikipedia.org/wiki/ Central_place_theory

70   See more at: www.aussietowns.com.au/town/poatina- tas#sthash.ttb90qxh.dpuf

71   Paul Sparks, Tim Soerens and Dwight J. Friesen (IVP, 2014)

72   Ray Simpson, *High Street Monasteries* (Kevin Mayhew, 2009)

73   Charles Plummer (ed., trans.), *Bethada Naem: Lives of IrishSaints* Vol. 2 (Forgotten Books, 2012)

74   See www.latrobe.edu.au/cssi/publications/cssi-newsletters/ issue-11-october-2014

75   See www.facebook.com/pages/Lighthouse-Central- Community-Hub-Project/1517696158509764?ref=hl

76   See www.causewaycoastvineyard.com

77   It seems that women worked their way into the Irish church scene gradually: they were not welcomed from the beginning. *The Catalogue of the Saints of Ireland*, written about the middle of the eighth century, states that the Second Order of Saints, which was influenced by the sixth-century Britons, 'rejected the ministry of women, banishing them from monasteries'. However, Oengus, in his ninth-century *Martyrology*, writing of 350 male saints of St Patrick's time, states that 'they rejected not the society and services of women'. Quoted in Peter Berresford Ellis, *Celtic Women: Women in Celtic society and literature* (Eerdman, 1995)

78   See Ray Simpson, *Hilda of Whitby: A spirituality for now* (BRF, 2014)

79   James Duffy, *St Ita, the Forgotten Princess* (Trafford, 2006)

80　'Life of Ita' in C. Plummer (ed.), *Vitae Sanctorum Hiberniae* (2 vols, 1968)

81　Stephanie Hollis, *Anglo-Saxon Women and the Church* (Boydell, 1992), p. 254

82　Quoted in Will Durant, *The Story of Philosophy: The lives and opinions of the world's greatest philosophers* (Pocket Books, 1991)

83　See Uinseann O'Maidin, *The Celtic Monk: Rules and writings of early Irish monks* (Cistercian Studies No. 162) (Cistercian Publications, 1996)

84　See Hugh Connolly, *The Irish Penitentials* (Four Courts, 1995)

85　Thomas Merton, *Disputed Questions* (Harcourt, 1985)

86　John C. Maxwell, *The 15 Invaluable Laws of Growth* (Center Street, 2014)

87　John O'Hanlon, *The Lives of the Irish Saints*, Vol. 8 (Forgotten Books, 2014)

88　See John O'Donovan (trans.), *The Martyrology of Donegal* (Forgotten Books, 2015), pp. 233, 261

89　www.aidanandhilda.org.uk

90　William Reeves (ed.), *Life of Saint Columba, Founder of Hy*, (HardPress, 2012), pp. 229–230

91　David Cole, *The Mystic Path of Meditation: Beginning a Christ-centred journey* (Harding House, 2013)

92　For the full text and commentary on the Aidan and Hilda Way of Life, see Ray Simpson, *A Pilgrim Way: New Celtic monasticism for everyday people, with study guide* (Kevin Mayhew, 2014)

93　Alasdair MacIntyre, *After Virtue* (University of Notre Dame Press, 1987)

94　Michael Frost, *The Road to Missional: Journey to the center of the church* (Baker Books, 2011), p. 28

95 See, for example, www.explorefaith.org/
    LentenHomily02.26.02.html

96 Richard Wilkinson and Kate Pickett, *The Spirit Level: Why
    equality is better for everyone* (Penguin, 2010)

97 Debra Green, *ROC Your World: Changing communities for good*
    (River Publishing, 2014)

98 James F. Cassidy, quoted in Hugh Graham, *The Early Irish
    Monastic Schools* (BiblioBazaar, 2009), p. 58

99 *The Sunday Age*, Melbourne (15 March 2015)

100 In Tony Cupit, Ros Gooden and Ken Manley (eds), *From
    Five Barley Loaves: Australian Baptists in global mission
    1864–2010* (Mosaic Press, 2011), p. 477

101 www.aidanandhilda.org.uk/about-way.php

102 Pope Francis (@Pontifex), Twitter, 16 May 2015

103 T.S. Eliot, *Christianity and Culture* (Harvest, 1960), p. 51

104 Joseph Barber Lightfoot, *Leaders in the Northern Church:
    Sermons preached in the diocese of Durham* (Macmillan, 1891)

105 www.raysimpson.org/userfiles/file/Clan_gathering_
    download_info.docx

106 For example, *The Independent* (23 April 2008) and *The
    Guardian* (29 January 2013)

107 See Ray Simpson, *The Lindisfarne Gospels: The English church
    and our multicultural world* (Kevin Mayhew, 2012)

108 Alfred Webb, *Compendium of Irish Biography* (M.H. Gill,
    1878)

109 http://johnmuirway.org/route

110 www.aberladyheritage.com

111 Bartram Colgrave and Brother Hermenegild TOSF, *Two Lives
    of Saint Cuthbert: A Life by an Anonymous Monk of Lindisfarne
    and Bede's Prose Life* (CreateSpace, 2013)

112 Ray Simpson, *Aidan of Lindisfarne: Irish flame warms a new
    world* (Wipf and Stock, 2014)

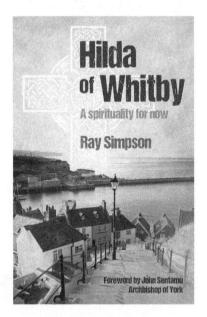

In the dark and turbulent centuries after the Roman occupation of Britain and during the Anglo-Saxon colonisation, the light of heaven still shone through the work and witness of the monastic communities, 'villages of God', which dotted the land. One of the most remarkable figures of those times was Hilda of Whitby. Born and reared among warring pagan tribes, through the influence of Celtic saints and scholars she became a dominant figure in the development of the British Church, above all at the famous Synod where Celtic and Roman Churches came together. Until recently, though, the story of this extraordinary woman has not received much attention.

This book not only explores the drama of Hilda's life and ministry but also shows what spiritual lessons we can draw for Christian life and leadership today.

Hilda of Whitby
A spirituality for now
Ray Simpson
ISBN 978 1 84101 728 0 £7.99

brf.org.uk